Conte

Digitox

How To Find A Healthy Balance For Your Family's Digital Diet

Mark Ellis

www.digitoxbook.com

CultureTransform

First published in the UK in 2017 by

CultureTransform Limited

www.culturetransform.com

ISBN Number 978-1-9997098-0-8

www.digitoxbook.com

For Caroline - my soulmate. The love of my life and the kindest, most talented, most generous and most beautiful person in the world.

Introduction

Thank you.

You're reading a book which I hope will change the way you think about the world, improve your life and make you (and your family) happier than you are at the moment. I don't know what you're expecting to find in here - but let's just checkbox what it's not.

This is not a book about the evils of technology. It's not a book about how to be a good person, or a good parent, or a good partner/wife/husband. This book will not outline a coherent strategy for fixing all that's wrong with your life, and (for the most part) will not rant about the modern world and it's perils.

This is a book in which I'll share our experiences of limiting the consumption of technology (in particular the flow of information from the internet) to myself and my family for the last three years. By doing so, I hope that you'll be encouraged to do the same while avoiding some of the pitfalls and screw-ups that happened to us.

I never set out to write a book about this, but more and more people kept telling me to share our story and what we've learned.

This is a book about dieting rather than giving up the internet, throwing the phone away or any one of a number of alternatives my friends gave me because that's exactly what it is - a diet.

Just like trying to lose weight - starvation, fad dieting or switching to cabbage soup for a week is not going to change behaviour long term. We went looking for a way to provide sustainable, regulated change that's easy to stick to as a lifestyle.

I can only offer advice, what you do with it is up to you. What I can tell you is that if you choose to follow this 'diet' you will think more clearly, improve your memory and teach yourself (and those around you) how to see the world with a little more clarity and connection. If you have children, then you'll find a lot less teenage tantrums happening, less grumpiness and a whole lot more positive interaction.

Oh, and don't expect instant results. Skipping the chocolate bar today won't make you slimmer tomorrow.

Part 1: Eating The Internet

This half of the book is about the effect that technology (and in particular the internet) has on our society, and why. The second half is all about us, although members of the family make frequent guest appearances in part one.

Progress

Change happens.

We need to change too, or we'll become extinct. After all, as Darwin said:

"It is not the strongest of the species that survives, nor the most intelligent that survives. It is the one that is most adaptable to change."

Actually he never said that. A professor from Louisiana State University named Leon Megginson said it at a convention in 1963, in reference to the Origin of The Species, but it's been attributed to Darwin ever since. As Abraham Lincoln once said, "Don't trust all you read on the internet."

Joking aside, fighting progress has been proved futile over and over again. In the early part of the 19th century, bands of English textile workers destroyed the machines that were taking their jobs. These were the 'Luddites' - an expression that lives on to describe people opposed to industrialisation or new technology.

Don't be a Luddite.
Nothing changed, the march of the machines continues. Most of us would be unhappy returning to horseback while our neighbours

drive cars.

I like to think that as a society we are somewhere between the steam age and the post-apocalyptic future represented by movies like "The Matrix" and "Terminator" - although sometimes when I see people using self-service checkout I have doubts - their head down, silent, phone in one hand and moving food over a scanner. Bleep. Bleep. Bleep.

One of the children I was at primary school with had parents who thought TV was a corrupting influence - I don't know what became of him, but he was seen as the 'weird' one by the rest of us because he couldn't talk about Fingermouse, Rainbow, Bagpuss or Sesame Street during break times.

No parent wants their children to be the odd ones out, which is part of the challenge posed here - some of the later chapters in this book will deal with this very issue, so don't worry about it just yet. Nothing that we've done personally has turned our children into social pariahs or outcasts.

The rate of technology change is accelerating exponentially - and it's a safe assumption that in some way or another we humans will remain plugged into both the archive (stuff that's already happened) and the flow (stuff that is happening now) of information collected by our species at an ever increasing rate.

This is a problem. The rate of data growth, and the rate of technology change far exceeds our historical ability to evolve, and that causes all kinds of mental and social challenges. Especially when coupled with the natural curiosity we possess as human beings.

My Wife is fond of drawing attention to the fact that all the labour saving devices (which began to proliferate in the 1960's) led to us needing to work harder and longer to afford them. A "keeping up with the neighbours" arms race if you will. The latest gadgets are just an extension of this evolution.

The way we access the internet has also become democratised - the premium smartphones, tablets, computers (and soon glasses) are still highly desirable, but the twin barriers of device and data costs have become low enough to allow access to the majority of those in the developed world.

Abraham Maslow's theory of human motivation, for 70 years the bastion of many a lecture on human psychology was updated several years ago to include wifi. Oh how we laughed at the thought that wifi could be more important than food, water, shelter and warmth.

Except that I am more likely to be anxious if I cannot find a wi-fi access point than if I cannot find a coffee, a snack, an umbrella or a coat.

Now it doesn't seem quite so funny.

Battery has since been added at the base of the triangle, which may explain why I need my external battery pack when I head out for the day, and the children expect one to be available wherever we go. Does this sound familiar to you?

So let me be absolutely clear - access to the internet is here to stay, it's normal, and this book is not going to try and talk anyone out of it - because that would be as dumb as throwing a clog into a weaving loom in an effort to stop industrial development.

It's Not Just About The Phone

"Great discoveries and improvements invariably involve the
cooperation of many minds. I may be given credit for having
blazed the trail, but when I look at the subsequent developments I
feel the credit is due to others rather than to myself"

Alexander Graham Bell

I am never alone, and neither are you - the world is saturated with
technology, and wholly reliant upon it. The sheer delight of
owning a personal device that allows you to talk with someone else
wherever you (or they) are has given way to a profound lack of
wonderment at the magic screen on the smartphone or tablet that
makes Star Trek seem like a technological backwater.

In 2010 less than 5% of pages loaded from the internet were
accessed using a mobile device. According to Statcounter research
that figure is now 51% - a trend which is not slowing down. Not
only is this the most popular way to access the web, it's the most
portable too.

In addition, there are approximately 7bn humans on Earth - and
6.8bn mobile phones. Think about that for a moment in terms of
the ratio of phone ownership to people.

Of course ownership is not evenly distributed - despite there being
enough for 97% of the planet's population Hong Kong has highest

ratio with 2.4 phones for every person. In the UK ownership is 130% (exactly the same as Iran) and in the USA it's slightly less at 103%

In fact only 19 countries have less than 100% ownership, and only three have less than 50% - Ethiopia (21%), Cuba (12%) and North Korea (8%). Whichever way you look at these figures - you can be assured that nearly everyone you know has access to a screen twenty four hours a day, seven days a week.

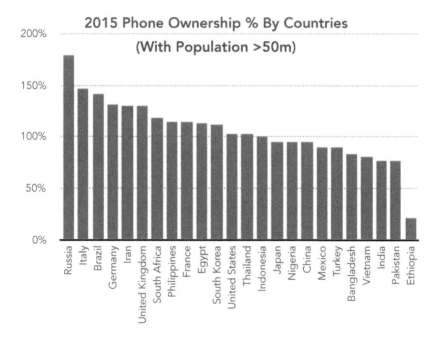

This is excluding personal computers. There are so many of those in circulation that we literally cannot measure the volume.

Gaming consoles have moved a long way from the original Atari style platforms, and now provide full scale immersive experiences that in almost all cases are permanently connected to the internet - in the last 20 years over 800 million units have shipped from Sony, Nintendo and Microsoft alone, yet another way that we remain connected to the world wide web.

In context, 46% of our planet have access to the internet and 65% have access to a toilet. The growth rate of internet access is far greater than the speed at which water sanitation is being extended - within the next seven years global internet access will outstrip sanitation access.

It's no wonder we see access to the internet as a necessity for survival. But it really is not.

Everything In Moderation

"Only actions give life strength; only moderation gives it charm"
Jean Richter

Before we start reducing consumption, I want to pause and draw attention to some of the wonderful and positive things that come from the internet, both for us personally and for society as a whole.

According to McKinsey the internet contributes 3.4% of gross domestic product (GDP) across thirteen countries, including the UK, the USA, Sweden and Japan, and actually helps create jobs - an analysis of job trends in France showed that while half a million jobs were lost due to the internet in the past 15 years, over 1.2 million have been created.

There are huge benefits to those over the age of 65 - moderate computer gaming improves memory, attention span and sequencing ability in old age - and virtual recreation programmes can improve health and fitness.

Our ability to communicate globally is taken for granted by my children. We can talk face to face with friends and colleagues all over the globe at little or no cost, and every time I FaceTime or Skype a friend in the USA I remember watching Star Trek as a child and marvelling at such a fantastical future vision. For senior citizens this is an invaluable way of reducing the sense of social isolation that accompanies the ageing process and loss of mobility.

Of course, when Tim Berners Lee created the foundations of the world wide web, it was intended to allow researchers to share information - that educational benefit now extends to online universities and continuous learning programmes, most noticeably the advent and popularity of massive open online courses (MOOCs) which count for over 35 million students enrolled in over 4,000 courses globally.

I was talking with a surgeon recently who can connect to operating theatres anywhere in the world, take control of surgical robots and save lives.

Before you recoil in horror at the idea of a robot messing about with your organs, remember that a full surgical team is still present on site, and the surgeon himself gets a greatly enhanced view of the procedure through massively magnified images. He also has microscopic control of his instruments - which leads to less intrusion, faster recovery rates and much improved long term outcomes.

Crowdfunding would be barely possible without the web. Accessibility for entrepreneurs to raise funds from small investors to get new ideas or products off the ground is only the tip of the iceberg in terms of benefits. Every day, thousands of ideas are improved, disproved, promoted or discarded through this medium which provides instant market research, promotion and funding at very low cost.

My family are involved in a community not for profit coffee shop, FLTR Coffee, which was funded by the generosity of local people and some distant friends. A large proportion of the money raised was made possible by the use of social media and a crowdfunding platform.

Not only did this provide our financial support, but also gave us the opportunity to engage people from the outset.

Why Diet?

Obesity is at epidemic proportions in the UK, and in the USA. According to a report from the National Institute of Diabetes & Digestive & Kidney Disease (**NIDDK**) 65% of the US population is obese or extremely obese. In the UK it's closer to 25% for obesity, and 62% for overweight.

This is now recognised as a problem, but until recent times obesity was seen as a sign of wealth - only the wealthy could afford enough food to become fat. What is truly shocking about the chart below is that only 6% of the US population are in the 'normal or underweight' category.

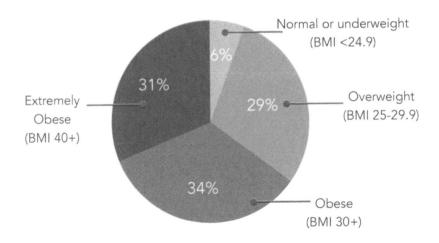

We can also draw some parallels between long-term learning from diet 🍎 and the short-term learning from internet 🌐 bingeing - specifically in relation to availability, age, education, exercise, marketing and expertise.

Availability

🍎 Inexpensive, high sugar, high fat options are widely available - leading to addiction.

🌐 Available almost everywhere. For the sake of argument let's assume you have access to wi-fi, 4G or networks if you want it 24 hours a day, 7 days a week. It's easier to get information than food or drink, and it's effectively 'free'.

Age

🍎 Obesity is more prevalent with younger children - a recent study in Birmingham showed 12% of the population overweight and 10% obese at age 5.

🌐 Younger people have less control than adults over their behaviour. This comes with it's own particular set of challenges - think of how much self-control a five year old has when faced with a giant bar of chocolate.

Education

Lower levels of education are directly correlated to higher levels of obesity.

Education was, and is the great promise of the internet. The ability to research, educate and connect - an incredible opportunity, but badly compromised by both data volume and temptation. Data volume means that checking facts becomes challenging, and reading beyond the first paragraph becomes time restrictive. In an ideal world we'd use the internet for noble reasons, but the distractions of games, time-waste sites, pornography and social media are competing in a way that can never happen in a physical library.

Exercise

Various factors contribute, tolerance to discomfort, availability of facilities, societal time pressures and significant diet changes necessary for physical health.

Our technology can help or hinder physical activity and fitness. Sitting and gazing at a screen vs using fitness trackers provides a very different outcome for our physical wellbeing.

Marketing

🍎 Economically, food companies drive much of their sales through advertising. This is especially true with children - where pester power works on parents, and chocolate sells better than flax bars and carrot sticks.

🌐 Open any web page, or any game on any device, and distractions abound. It benefits to have in-game purchases, and every web site is competing not only for your attention now, but to keep that attention for as long as possible before earning revenue from your 'click through' behaviours.

Expertise

🍎 For years we've been told that fat and sugar are harmful. Low fat spread and diet drinks are better - the end result is dysmorphic body shapes and heart disease. The reality is that everything should be consumed in moderation - but that's a message that doesn't seem to play well in our modern society.

🌐 Expertise is still developing, but common sense, facts and science paint a very clear picture. Much of this is discussed right here in the book you're reading.

As we move through this book, visualise technology use (in particular internet consumption) as a flow of food. Nutritionally balanced diets are great - but temptations abound.

It is easy to assume that the internet is free, but it is the opportunity cost (the value of what we could be doing instead) that is the real problem - and common sense should tell you that too much of anything is not good for you, be that food or technology.

A friend of mine took his son, aged eleven to a squash court recently - in an effort to extract him from the living room at home. Twenty minutes into playing, he (not his father) was out of breath and begging for a break.

My friend pointed out to him that when he was eleven, he could have literally run around all day to which the reply was "Yes, but you didn't have access to the internet when you were young".

Ouch.

I would add that before the trip to the leisure centre, there were arguments about wanting to spend two hours on the computer instead. After playing, squash games have become a regular occurrence - at the insistence of the former eleven year old couch potato himself.

The Four Pillars

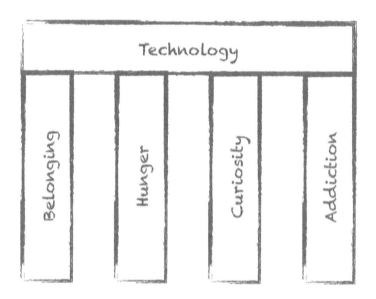

As a family, we have identified four distinct areas that underpin our use of technology (and in particular the internet). This has provided the 'perfect storm'. These are:

Belonging

We all like to 'fit in' - peer pressure is a key motivator in human behaviour, while the urge to have the most modern, up to date object can be put down to a number of other factors - the fact is that we are programmed at a genetic level to be part of the 'tribe'.

Sixty years ago the tribe started to buy refrigerators, dishwashers, food mixers, washing machines, and even early televisions. Right now status within the tribe is defined by the age and size of their large screen HDTV, smartphones, computers, laptops, gadgets and cars.

In the last decade, kitchen and home appliances have been replaced by portable gadgets - many of which are annually updated as the pace of technology increases. Here are my picks of 'must have' gadgets from the last ten years - most of which are still in use today, and only the eldest has no native internet connection.

Interestingly enough, one tribal behaviour that was prevalent a decade ago has subsided - the discussion of 'last nights TV'.

Streaming of programs through 'catch up' channels and a on-demand suppliers have now become widely adopted. In the UK alone there are six million subscribers to Netflix, Amazon and Sky Now, and over 19 million adults used the BBC iPlayer (an online catch up service) in the last twelve months.

If you don't belong to the tribe, you have to live on the outside of the social structure. Just like the child whose parents didn't allow TV, depriving yourself (or your offspring) access to a smartphone , a tablet or the internet is seen as 'odd'.

This underpins a significant challenge when you try and restrict your access to something that the rest of the tribe is doing - there will be considerable peer pressure to give in. How often do you hear "Everyone else is doing it" from your children, or from your own colleagues and friends?

Hunger

What happens when you eat too much? The bag that holds your food (your stomach) expands, and the next day you need just a little bit more to feel full. Reduce food intake for a few days, and the reverse is true.

The more we indulge in technology, the more our brain creates an internal requirement for more. Couple this with the human desire to learn, and the perfect psychological storm occurs - the more we do something we like, the more we want to do it.

Not only is the brain creating this requirement, it's also rewiring itself to expect it. Within the brain neurons line up in chains depending on our daily activity - effectively joining up brain cells to make the processing of information easier and faster. This is called Neuroplasticity.

The longer you spend performing a behaviour, the stronger the impulse to continue doing it, and the harder the habit to break. The good news is that your brain can be rewired regardless of age - if you can overcome the impulses that encourage you to repeat the same behaviours.

Curiosity

We all know what curiosity did to the cat. As Ellen Parr (not Dorothy Parker) once said "The cure for boredom is curiosity, there is no cure for curiosity".

The internet is a curious person's nightmare or fantasy, depending on personal outlook. Anyone can find anything (if you know where to look) and often you will find things that you don't want to know, never asked for and were never looking for. The world of internet marketing relies on the power of distraction and curiosity to make money.

Facebook Advertising Revenue By Quarter
2014-2016 ($m)

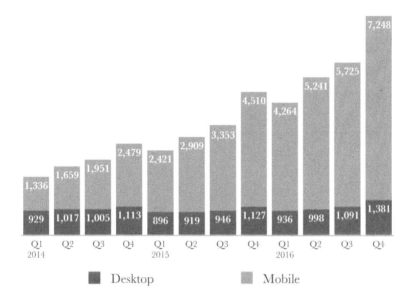

Desktop   Mobile

Almost every website you visit has a commercial reason for existence, and that means it needs to be self sustaining. Take Facebook as an example, and their spectacular growth from advertising revenue alone shown in the chart.

That's $26 billion dollars of revenue in 2016 from advertising. At the start of 2017 there were 1.86bn active users, that's $14 of advertising for every user. More Facebook users, spending more time on Facebook equates to more money for Facebook.

That's good business, but it does mean that there's a huge number of really smart people trying to distract you online with an advert, and stop you getting back on with whatever it is you should be doing instead. Also don't lose sight of the fact that around 84% of this revenue came from mobile users.

There is a more sinister side to this. Several years ago one of my friends returned from a business trip to find his 8 year old son asleep in bed. He was disturbed to find that a tablet was resting on the covers, and slid it out from between the hands of the sleeping child.

Curious to see what his son had been reading, he pushed the button to bring the screen back to life.

And found to his horror that a necrophilia scene was playing out in front of him. He took seven clicks backwards and found that his son had started this journey from an ad banner at the side of Facebook (which was perfectly legal), and continued on from there.

There's a short section on parental controls at the back of the book if this is something that you are interested in. I'd suggest that if you have children of any age, you should seriously consider them.

Addiction

Too much of almost anything leads to addiction. The endless search for the 'bigger hit' occurs with almost everything - that can be chocolate, alcohol, gaming, drugs, pornography, and yes, that includes technology and the internet.

The perfect storm of belonging, hunger and curiosity lead inevitably to an internet addicted society. In the unlikely event that you are displaying no addictive behaviour at all, that's fantastic - but those around you are likely suffering to a greater or lesser extent from the problem, and in just a few short chapters we're going to look at how to spot that, and what to do about it.

Four Pillars - Four Takeaways

Belonging - the tribal gadgets do not define you as a person, but communication with your tribe often requires the use of the internet.

Hunger - bingeing the internet is harmful to your brain and mental health in much the same way as bingeing food is harmful to your physical health.

Curiosity - human curiosity drives advertising and marketing that keeps you both engaged and distracted, and companies invest a lot of money to keep you connected.

Addiction - the first three pillars transform something which is naturally attractive into a recipe for becoming addicted to technology and in particular the internet (just like almost everyone in your tribe)

Information Overload

"Noise does not cancel out noise, silence does"
Mahatma Gandhi

According to EMC, 1.7mb of new information will be created every second for every human being on the planet by 2020.

Impressive stuff, but hang on, what exactly is a mb? What does that actually mean?

Well 1.7 megabytes would be a mid sized photo taken on your phone, and there are 7bn people on Earth. So that's 7bn photos per second being gathered. 1.7mb is also roughly the same size as an electronic book - so that's 7bn books per second of information being created.

What are we going to do with all this? We store it 'just in case' it's needed in the future and the smart people at Google will work out how to index and catalog the entire internet for us so we can find what we need.

You can never see it all, but the pressure of all that knowledge out there is a huge attraction. Whatever it is that you want to see or learn about - you can probably find it out there. Good, bad or mediocre.

Remember our diet - there's information chocolate and information kale out there - which do you pursue? What are your children likely to pursue, or those around you?

1.4bn smartphones will be shipped this year - packed with sensors collecting information that you (and others) can use to predict behaviour, tailor marketing and so much more.

How many of us are plugged into the social media sweet shop? It's almost impossible to tell, but current statistics show that the number of active users on the most popular platforms are:

Facebook 1.9bn

YouTube 1bn

Google+ 540m

Instagram 500m

Twitter 319m

Snapchat 300m

Weibo 260m

Placed in context more than a quarter of the population of planet Earth are active on Facebook.

In the USA alone, in a single minute, the weather channel website receives nearly 14m requests for forecasts, 2.5m photographs get 'liked' on Instagram, 3.5m text messages are sent, and 18m megabytes of wireless data are used. That is a staggering, and I'm only scratching the surface here.

Why is this important? It means that the taps are always on. The information never ever stops. There is <u>always</u> something new to see, an update to check or a photo to 'like'. This is not good, it's the equivalent of a nagging child that will never, ever be quiet. We are drowning and we've yet to find an effective method of swimming, or even treading water.

Managing Sleep

"The amount of sleep required by the average person is five minutes more." - Wilson Mizener

Do you take your phone upstairs when you go to bed? Do you bring into the bedroom? Do you put it on the bed? If you do, then you're part of the majority. My excuse is that my charging station (also my alarm clock/stereo) is next to the bed. This is not good enough.

Four things to bear in mind about bringing your phone to bed.

1 Number one, if you look at it within half an hour of trying to get to sleep you will prevent melatonin increase. This is a hormone you need to sleep. The backlight blue and green of your screen does a great job in preventing this from happening, and 'brightness' and 'night' settings only help a little.

2 Two - the sleep you do get is not great. Staying up later messes with your body clock and something called 'delayed sleep phase syndrome' set's in. Effectively your body creates a sleep pattern that is very hard to break, when you consistently fall asleep at 1am, it becomes very hard to change that.

3   Wi-fi is not good for you. Really not good for you - and placing the phone with wi-fi on near your head all night is only going to increase the exposure to the low level radiation it's emitting.

4   Four - and this is one we'll revisit, FOMO. Or fear of missing out. You mind cannot rest when you are in an expectant state - i.e. waiting for a text or email to chime, you may think that you are not doing this, but subconsciously this is how your mind is acting. Facebook activity happens 24 hours a day, and your brain knows it. Scientifically this is known as a state of hyper-vigilance - this is something that those with post traumatic stress disorder can suffer from. This makes you constantly on guard, tense and anxious - and is caused by being subconsciously alert for incoming phone calls, emails or text messages.

Oh yes - and according to a study by Harris Interactive and Jumio 20% of young adults are on the phone during sex.

If that's you, then you have many more problems than this book can help you with! But while we're talking about this, a substantial number of studies have shown that leaving the phone outside the bedroom leads to an improvement in your sex life. This is a statistic more exaggerated in women than in men.

So the very first thing you should do is stop using your phone at least thirty minutes before you go to bed. Give your brain the chance to relax, your melatonin the chance to increase, and drift off to sleep naturally and easily.

If you have a fitness device with a heart monitor, you can test this for yourself. Compare a week when you take your phone to the bedroom against going without and you'll notice that your sleep/ wake /restless patterns are better and your resting heart rate is likely to be lower too.

Needless to say this is not going to work if your heart monitor is connected to your phone, and can also receive endless text messages, emails and alerts.

One more thing.

'Backlit' e-readers are often not actually backlit, but project light onto the screen sideways, not directly into your eyes. Keeping the light levels low will minimise the melatonin inhibition, although using a clip-on or bedside light can still better be for you. So if you're reading this on your Kindle Paperwhite, don't panic.

If you are using a device with a screen, and you don't want to give up reading before sleeping, then consider switching back to actual paper, or a dedicated e-reader.

Motivation

"The pessimist sees difficulty in every opportunity.
The optimist sees the opportunity in every difficulty"
Winston Churchill

Who has fun on a diet? Nobody. I suppose there are few people out there who like to feel hungry, enjoy levels of self control or fast for spiritual purposes, but I for one do not like the experience of going without enough food.

So how do we even start motivating for a diet? When your belt gets tight, your breathing gets harder or you just don't like the look of yourself in the mirror, that's usually a significant catalyst for change.

Support groups work well. It's been proven over many decades that diet clubs work, but there is no "TechnologyWatchers" group in my area to support me.

And that's the challenge with starting to restrict internet and gadget access, we found it was very hard to justify starting this progress - it just 'felt right' to see if we could reduce our time online (the second half of the book deals with the run up to this 'feeling' and what happened next) - with the benefit of hindsight, we now have some tangible family results, and a much better lifestyle.

A few years ago my dad patted my stomach, and told me that I was bulging over my belt (he may have been a little less tactful). That did it for me, I started to exercise more and eat less. So why, when someone asks you to 'put the phone down' or 'put the laptop away' do you respond so badly? Why does this happen when you ask your children the same thing?

It's because you're addicted. You really are - but you may not think it, so I'm now going to try and prove to you that you are with a few simple tests.

Addiction

"I can choose to let it define me, confine me, refine me, or outshine me, or I can choose to move on, and leave it behind me."

Unknown

Did you know that 'addiction' comes from the Latin for 'enslaved by'?

On the first day we decided to go tech free, I was shocked by the feelings that stirred in me and the attitude of my family. It was horrible - there were arguments, plea's for exceptions, shouting - and it left us all exhausted. I'm stubborn though, and because of this reaction we carried on.

But why did we react this way? Why did the children fall out? Why was this such a major event? Simple. We were all addicted to a greater or lesser extent.

The definition of internet addiction its a slippery one - put simply there is no clear marker for how many hours per day constitutes 'addicted'. It varies by person, and although there is a nominal 'more than 3 hours per day' statement typically used, scientific evidence points to the actual number of hours being lower than that.

There are some simple tests to try - but first ask yourself how addicted you believe you are to the following things (and feel free to add your own devices to the list).

Television

Radio

Smartphone

Tablet

Computer

Kindle

Next rank them in their order of importance (to you) - with the one you would give up first at the bottom, and the one you couldn't live without at the top. Be honest with yourself.

In my case, the answer to this became abundantly clear a few years back as I prepared to go on a business trip to Germany. That morning my phone requested an update, which I 'approved' and then went about my business - but it didn't work out well.

As I collected my bags and placed them in the car, I returned to get the phone only to find that the update hadn't worked properly - and my phone was now back to 'new' state, with none of my apps, games, email or preferences stored. I'd love to say I responded calmly and rationally, but I threw a shouty fit worthy of a hormonal teenager.

You see my flight tickets were there, my email instructions for the taxi, the hotel directions, my e-books, my games, my news, my weather. How could I cope venturing on a business trip without these things! Running madly to my laptop I printed out the flight tickets, ran to the car and started the hour long drive to London while continuing my tantrum.

Retrospectively it was a truly embarrassing episode, I was shaking, yelling and stressed when the reality was that my laptop had all the information I needed held within, and my smart phone was reduced to the role of 'telephone' for a couple of days (until I returned home and restored the backup). The world had NOT stopped turning.

A few months later I had my laptop stolen in the middle of a conference I was hosting in Barcelona. A device I needed for creating my slides, checking my notes and performing my social media broadcast duties.

Same reaction? Nope, not a bit. I had to jump onto stage five minutes after it disappeared and although I was a little stressed, I could put it to one side - lean back on my notebook and pen and deliver the next two days without it. When I got home, my insurance provided replacement was waiting, and the backup restored perfectly.

So for me (as for so many others) the device I really could not manage without was the smartphone. Absurd, except of course, I was addicted to it, or at least to the things it enabled me to do.

Viewed through the lens of addiction, my reaction was not so unexpected after all.

There have been a number of studies to determine what internet addiction is, how many hours per day need to be exceeded to become an addict and what behaviour patterns should be recognised. Scientifically it's a tough one - as we're all different, our compulsions vary, as do our desires and interests. For some, 30 minutes per day is enough to develop an addiction, in others it can be as much as 3 hours per day - younger minds are more vulnerable.

As yet there is no simple formula for determining this, although based on the studies that have been completed, if you're spending more than two hours per day online then you are an addict.

I'm not going to set out the deep psychological implications or cognitive impacts in great detail just yet, for now I'd ask you to accept that this is a real condition, and it's just as harmful as any other addiction.

On the other hand, alcohol, drug and food addictions are well understood, so next I am going to ask you some questions about your behaviour with regard to technology and the internet. You can include almost anything in this - gaming, news surfing, social media, YouTube - it's entirely personal.

There is a standard three part test for determining a drug or alcohol addiction - do you:

1 Crave the object of addiction
2 Suffer loss of control over its use
3 Continue involvement despite adverse consequence

Craving The Object Of Addiction

So - do you crave the object of addiction? If you couldn't find it when you 'needed' it - would it bother you? Paint yourself a mental picture of not being able to find your smartphone tomorrow, or waking up to find the internet unavailable. What would you do?

Let's not be quite so catastrophic - let's say I asked you sit at a table with your smartphone on it. Your job is not to look at it or touch it. You would be surprised at how hard that is for some people.

My Wife spends time working with teenage girls, in a programme through our local Church which deals with issues facing younger people today - from self-harming through eating disorders and body issues. One of our priests used to be a beautician, and during the six weeks the girls learn all kinds of nail manicure techniques too.

Sometimes during discussions, the girls are all asked to place their phones on the table they are gathered around and leave it alone. It typically takes less than a minute before someone reaches out for theirs. Often they are not even conscious of the behaviour.

During another youth group, while viewing Gary Turk's "Look Up" video poem, most of the teens could not sit and watch for more than a few moments before anxiety set in and they became noticeably agitated, glancing repeatedly at their phones placed tantalisingly out of reach.

Take a look around you next time you're out - and see how many people cannot leave their phone alone for more than sixty seconds. If this is you, then you have a problem. Is there anyone in your family who unconsciously reaches for their gadget at every opportunity?

If so, then you're seeing the manifestation of an addiction.

If this was someone you loved and they were reaching for a drink, craving the bottle, or the joint, or the needle, or even the chocolate cake, would you accept the behaviour and not offer some help?

Loss Of Control Over Its Use

This is a tougher one to work out, and you have to be completely honest with yourself. My eldest son (Ben) has a propensity for gaming addiction (as do I), he imagined that he could spend fifteen minutes on Minecraft with his friends, and then get on with homework. Several hours later and he would still be playing - that 'time slip' is an easy identifier for a problem.

Procrastination is the act of delaying or postponing something - and the internet supports our internal desire to do this. It is the ultimate in temptation - access to the web provides a multitude of distractions and this limits our ability to think clearly.

Ben often remarks that his relaxation is reliant on taking a break and diving into Imgur, or Minecraft or (insert your favourite here), and while studies show that taking a break is critical to effective work - control over that time spent is even more important.

We were talking recently, and he told me that he'd installed an application on his laptop called "Cold Turkey" - which allows him to set barriers to many of the things that distract him from his studies. Once in place, there is no way of 'unblocking' until the time limit you set is reached. He knows he has to work hard to get his University place, and has enough self-awareness to understand the potential damage his addiction to the internet could cause him.

I don't believe that this self awareness, or the ability to do something about it would have been there if not for our diet programme.

One of the biggest challenges for teens at the moment is the collection of 'virtual internet points'. This is the accumulation of 'likes', 'comments' or 'streaks' gained in the social media arena.

For most younger social media users, it's normal to make a post (words, pictures or both) and then check regularly to see how much attention it has been gathering. If the requisite amount of attention is not gained, then the post is likely to be changed or deleted.

Take a moment and think about that. Older tech users have been conditioned by the 'fire and forget' mentality of email. Yes, conversation may ensue - but that email is out of your mind.

For younger tech users, email is not the primary method of communication, social media, instant messaging and photo sharing are used. These things can be changed or removed at will (for the most part) and so anxiety sets in and posts are regularly checked - they are never 'out of mind'.

There are over 939,000 posts every minute of every day on Facebook, 350,000 Tweets on Twitter and 56,000 photos uploaded to Instagram. All collect likes, all can be deleted or changed - all consume multiple revisits.

Think about the brain space that takes up. Is that person in control? I'd argue not - in fact I'd argue that the level of behaviour modification caused by this, and the normalising of that within society is a challenge for all of us. It's the High School popularity challenge raised to extreme levels.

Again, ask yourself if you or anyone you know has a control issue around their technology. We certainly did.

Continuing Involvement Despite Adverse Consequence

This is easily visible in an alcoholic or a drug addict - the loss of self control, the behaviour change caused by dependency and the change in personality is well documented and well understood. What about the technology space though?

Let's start by looking at 'adverse consequence'. Starting at the extreme end.

In July 2015 a web site called Ashley Madison was hacked. This was a business who's tag line was "Life's short, have an affair" - and 32 million people had their details released to the public with at least three suicides directly attributed to that. In April 2016,

Beautiful People shared the same fate, in October 2016 412m users had their details leaked after "Adult Friend Finder" was hacked.

Documented adverse consequences of internet addiction include suicide, divorce, car accidents and poor examination results. In 2016, 50% of divorce hearings stated online porn use as a reason, there were 430,000 car accidents in America in 2012 attributed to phone distraction, and teachers are reporting poor examination results due to time spent gaming, surfing and 'chatting' instead of in study or revision.

For the last decade, pornographic viewing habits have formed a basis for thousands of dismissals from work, wether that be live viewing of movies, surfing images or storing images on computers at the office. During my time in the software industry this bewildered me, not just on moral and decency grounds - but also due to the astonishing level of naivety.

There are many ways to uncover employees looking at porn - logging browsing behaviours against black lists, examination of incoming images for 'skin' coloured pixels, staff reporting strange noises from colleagues and so on.

Don't forget it's in the best interest of any employer to do this, not only for time wasted and lack of productivity - but also for the risks posed in terms of complaints and legal action from fellow employees affected by seeing this stuff on the screens of others.

Your adverse results may be different - in my case it was looking around at the family and realising that the technology we used was creating distance between us - with each member of the family on a varying scale of addiction to different things and some early warning signs of communication challenges.

I have friends who have lost jobs because of social media addiction, I've had to talk with employees about pornography viewing in the workplace and I've had to physically remove technology from my children after uncovering them abusing my trust.

I would hope that none of this has happened to you, or anyone you know - but it is statistically unlikely to be the case.

Internet Addiction

In May 2013, Internet gaming disorder (IGD) was included in reports from the American Psychiatric Association as a condition warranting further study. While this was specific to internet gaming it does have wider implications (and is often referred to as Internet Use Disorder or IUD). The criteria used for classification and study were as follows:

• Preoccupation with Internet games

• Withdrawal symptoms of irritability, anxiety, or sadness

• Development of tolerance (the need to spend more time gaming)

• Unsuccessful attempts to control the behaviour

• Loss of interest in other activities

• Continued excessive use despite knowledge of psychosocial problems

• Deceiving others regarding the amount of time spent gaming

• Use of this behaviour to escape or relieve a negative mood

• Jeopardising/losing a significant relationship/job/educational opportunity

I have observed every single one of these in my household, and the same applies for many of my friends. Yet in most cases the behaviour remains unchecked.

So now it's time for the tough questions, are you (or your family) showing warning signs of an addiction, or are you actually addicted already? Taking the last test one step further, how many of these sound familiar?

Internet Addiction Warning Signs   Y/N

Do you have thoughts about previous online activity, or are you actively anticipating your next session? ☐

Do you spend more time connected to the internet than you used to, in order to gain the same amount of satisfaction? ☐

Have you tried before to stop using your phone / the internet / another gadget - and failed. ☐

If you cut down your use, do you notice an increase in irritability, moodiness or even depression? ☐

Does time 'slip away from you' online? ☐

Do you use the internet to escape from reality - when you are online do you feel less anxiety? ☐

Honesty is key here - I know that I have an addictive personality, so it's easy for me to hold up my hand and say "this is me" - and I can certainly spot this in some of my children, but not all.

Physical Harm

Alcoholics damage their liver, obese people damage their hearts, internet addicts damage their brains. You may think that I'm talking about neural pathway changes, or alterations in learned behaviour - but I'm not, there are physical indicators that the longer adolescents spend on line, the more damage they do to their brains.

A number of recent studies have shown that there are physical effects on the brain in adolescents - the most comprehensive (and frightening) are the results of neuro-imaging findings in internet and gaming addiction by Lin & Zhou et al in 2012. Which showed (amongst other things):

• Grey matter atrophy - Grey matter is where processing occurs, and shrinkage and tissue loss here included the frontal lobe - that part of the brain concerned with impulse control, organisation, prioritisation and planning.

• Compromised white matter integrity - this causes loss of connection between hemispheres and brain centres - effectively limiting communication between different areas of the brain.

• Impaired cognitive function - causing lower impulse inhibition, increased sensitivity to rewards and insensitivity to loss. Abnormal activity leading to poor task performance was also noted as part of the study.

• Cravings - as dopamine is released during gaming, brain changes can be observed physically that are similar to drug cravings. Heavy internet users showed reduced numbers of dopamine receptors and transporters.

There's a temptation to disregard research as not applicable, inconsistent or far fetched. When I spoke to Ben (our eldest) about this, he dismissed it as fantastical and improbable. He may have come up with some other words too - but he wasn't going to accept it in a typical addicts response.

I explained to him that if you put somebody in an MRI machine and scan their lungs for signs of damage, and you do this to enough people, you can derive a correlation between smokers and lung disease.

What Fuchu Lin and his colleagues did was conduct the same process on the brains of adolescents. They observed a correlation between 'time spent on the internet' and 'damage to the brain'.

The full report cites sixty-nine references to external work, has been peer reviewed, and published across the world. You can distill all this research into one simple, basic truth, especially among adolescents:

more time on the web = more brain damage

Addiction Takeaways

1. Internet addiction is personal, there is no specific number of hours per day that classifies anyone as an internet addict, although most studies suggest that greater than three hours is a good indicator.

2. It is a natural defence to deny being addicted, and we are conditioned by our society to assume that internet access is benign.

3. If you crave the internet, suffer loss of personal control when you use it, and continue using it despite adverse consequence - you are addicted (at some level).

4. Addiction causes physical harm to the brain regardless of age, but is more acute in adolescents.

Instant Gratification

"The ability to discipline yourself to delay gratification in the short term in order to enjoy greater rewards in the long term is the indispensable prerequisite for success."

Maxwell Maltz

There is one final part of the addiction recipe that needs addressing - the concept of instant gratification.

As a society, we have become much more focused on 'now'. This is nothing new - in ancient Egypt craftsmen took years to complete single statues, in the 1800's chairs took weeks to make, now modern manufacturing techniques mean that I can make one in minutes (thank you Ikea for creating the kit).

When my parents moved into their house, they sat on tea chests, and slept on the floor. When we moved into our house 20 years ago it took us nearly three years before every room had curtains. Now the expectation is for perfect show home style decoration from day one.

This drive for 'now' has meant an explosion of credit debt - but more importantly has evolved into a lack of patience when it comes to any form of gratification. Think about how people used to learn, when I was in the middle of my degree I spent most of my time in the library putting together papers and essays - learning around the subject. If I needed to cross reference news, then I headed to a microfiche machine (try explaining what one of those is to someone under the age of 30).

Access to the internet has made this a much easier, richer process - but with that explosion of information and data, there is a level of 'filtering' done leading to only the most popular content hitting the top of the search engine, which in turn creates its own problems.

But that's not the real issue - although research can be done with the small screen in your pocket, it's still easier to sit down with a keyboard. The portable distraction machine means that the need to wait or think is dramatically diminished. What's the weather going to be like later? Who's that actor in the film? What is that song playing? The answer is only a click away - but that's not necessarily a healthy habit to develop.

While society focuses on impulsiveness and short term gain - so we as individuals start down the same route. This has an effect on brain structure, in particular with regard to decision making and self-control. One of the first things we noticed as a challenge to spending time away from the tech, was the internal chatter of "I want to know this" that could no longer be satisfied.

Test yourself. Don't try and give up everything. Think about something you do multiple times a day that you enjoy - it could be a quick game on the phone, or checking the weather, or reading the news headlines. Then try and stop doing it.

So how do you stop? If you were trying to lose weight by eating less, you might identify chocolate as something that provides short term instant gratification.

•Be Self Aware - when the thought crosses your mind that chocolate would be nice, recognise the urge for what it is. Not a need, but a want. Feel like checking Instagram, need or want? You decide.

•Exercise a small degree of self-control. Delay the urge for the short term - you may find it goes away as the rational part of your thought process takes over. You may not - but placing that 'pause' helps you recognise that you actually don't need a sugar rush, or indeed to know what the weather will be like in the next hour.

•Make a rational, conscious decision. If you haven't eaten in hours, you're feeling light headed, and a chocolate bar will help you stop having hunger anger - go for it. Just don't obey the urge, place some thought in the way. Likewise, it can be rational to check for incoming snow on a forecast before setting out on a long car journey.

•Accept that you'll slip. But after you eat the chocolate bar, realise you didn't need it, and feel guilty - focus on that feeling. What can you learn? What led you to stuff your face? When your wife glares at you across the table for picking up the phone during dinner - what are the long term-consequences of your actions?

- Enjoy the moment - if you skip the chocolate and you know you made the right decision, give yourself a pat on the back. Often we don't see what's around us for the urges we give into. Instead of walking around with eyes down on the phone, who knows what you might see out in the world. Who knows what you may be missing?

Pornography

This is the most difficult part of the book to write. It's tough for me to address this one, and I don't even want to research it. Why? Because I'm male, and of course I've explored the internet pornography world in the past. I don't like that I did, and I quickly realised it was an unhealthy place to be.

I'm also a husband, a father and a Christian - and to be honest this makes this more than a little uncomfortable to talk about. Before we move on though, I'm going to do a little historical scene setting.

Nudity and sex have been good business for a very long time. Prostitution is not called the oldest profession for nothing (Rudyard Kipling coined that particular phrase in 1888).

I was born in 1972, and my first exposure to naked lady pictures was in the school library, where along with all similar minded boys (meaning everyone) - I knew the location of every 'art' book with inappropriate imagery. From there it was a short step to the black market in second-hand Playboy magazines from the older kids -

and by the time I reached University several worn out video tapes were doing the rounds.

If I wanted any more exposure to this stuff, then I needed to head to a newsagent and reach up to the top shelf, then buy it at the counter. Not the easiest thing for an embarrassed teenager (and I never did dare) - or even worse, find a sex shop somewhere.

I'm a bit of technical geek, and so it's not unusual for other parents to ask me questions about this, and on occasion I've done some quick forensic work to allow them to see what their children are looking at on line.

Without exception, parents of roughly my age imagine that little Johnny is looking at the same kind of stuff that they were. Perhaps a tasteful picture of Cindy Crawford naked on a rug, or maybe, just maybe a couple of people engaged in some of the more sober extracts from the Karma-Sutra.

I'm telling you now that this is not the case.

Just like the tale of the eight year old finding necrophilia images through his tablet, the ever escalating war of attraction means that pornography needs to become more extreme, harder and more shocking to gain more visitors. The visitors pay directly, or in the form of adverts, and competition is fierce. Internet porn is a $97bn industry.

This means that adult and child alike are victim to the same pull as any addict - we keep needing the harder drugs or the bigger hit.

After insisting that the parents sat with me as I went through their sons computer, they were horrified to find that Miss Crawford was nowhere in sight, but there were plenty of images of women tied to beds, gang rape, strangulation and even horses.

Think again about parental controls and the balance of 'privacy' to 'parenting'.

What's the most popular pornography on the web? It's hard to determine, but one popular site recently released some statistics from it's users. I stress that this is a 'mainstream' site, and among it's top searches were gangbang, step sister, step dad and daughter, anal, scissoring and teen.

Fast growing pornography in the 'darker' areas of the web includes rape and strangulation porn (and much worse that I am NOT going to cover here, and wish I had never found out about).

Now connect that with the fact that one popular porn website reported 23bn visits per year, and 4.5bn hours of porn watched.

One site - let that sink in. 12% of sites on the web are pornographic, and a quarter of all search engine requests. 35% of all downloads are pornographic.

Stop and ponder those facts for a moment.

I want you to think about two much more relevant and critical parts of this puzzle. One - pornography is addictive, highly addictive - the nude pictures first viewed provide a dopamine rise to the brain, but (just as with drugs) the brain adapts and requires more and more potent (extreme) images to provide the same level of pleasure.

And two - anyone with a smartphone has access to the internet.

No sneaking to the library, no braving newsagents or sex shops. No control and no filter - want to guess what kids are sharing on their phones at school? And trust me, the most shocking images and videos are the ones that get the most attention.

Oh - and you're not going to stop it either. Even with parental controls on your child's phone, others won't have it. So it's time for those tough conversations to happen.

BUT you can do something about it - and that's block it at home. Unless something changes dramatically, extensive viewing of pornography is not often a group activity - and solitary time generally happens at home. So limit the data plan, and get the controls put in place.

"We have to tell our kids that pornographic sex is fake and real sex is about love, not lust."

Martin Daubney

The Distraction Challenge

"Work is hard. Distractions are plentiful. And time is short."
Adam Hochschild

Distraction is not a 'youth' problem, it affects every generation. In a study by AVG Technologies 32% of children felt unimportant when their parents were distracted by their phones.

I did not need a study to tell me this, when my friends glance at their phones (or smart watches) during conversation I feel pretty unimportant too. So sorry, am I boring you?

54% of children think that their parents spend too much time on the phone. Adults set the example here, and I'm afraid that statistically it's not a good one - especially as hypocritically a quarter of parents in the same survey said they wished their children used their own devices less.

But let's not worry about that. Distraction during conversation is rude, but rarely fatal - instead let's look at the number of deaths every year that result from smart devices in moving vehicles. Unless you have your phone turned off in the car (and I don't know anyone that does) - statistically speaking you are removing some of your attention from the road ahead of you.

At least one in four car accidents are caused by mobile phone use, a number which is far lower than reality. At this time phones are only seized by police in the UK following accidents resulting in fatal or life threatening injury - although you can expect to have your phone taken away for forensic examination following any road incident. The data will describe exactly what you were doing during the journey, and that evidence is submissible in court.

This is tough behaviour to curb, as many people use their phones as navigation devices (as did I) - and as a consequence they are placed in plain sight, and not always correctly secured - either physically or electronically (in terms of alerts).

In 2016, less than 10 miles from where we live Tomasz Kroker drove his truck into the back of a stationary car on the A34 near Oxford. Tracy Houghton, 45, her sons, Ethan, 13, Josh, 11, and stepdaughter, Aimee, 11 were killed instantly by the 50mph impact. Tomasz was scrolling through music on his phone at the time, less than one hour after signing a declaration with his employer that he would not use a mobile phone at the wheel.

It is likely he was completely unaware of his abnormal behaviour, as with so many of the habits we develop. At the scene, he broke down crying, saying "I've killed them". On the 31st October 2016 he was sentenced to ten years in prison.

There is a very successful campaign in America to stop drivers using their phones behind the wheel, founded by AT&T the "It Can Wait" pledge has been taken by over 14 million drivers, in a response to the staggering statistic that over 430,000 crashes were caused by drivers distracted at the wheel every year.

Hands free calling is not necessarily the solution - a study by the American Automobile Association on cognitive distraction researched the effect that using voice commands to a phone or car had on reaction times (to make a call, send a text or change music). It showed that on average, it took 27 seconds for a drivers reaction times to return to normal 'undistracted' levels.

Walking along, or sitting at your desk using Siri, Cortana, Google Assistant or Alexa will also cause cognitive distraction, but as you are not in control of several tons of speeding metal, is less likely to cause a fatality.

Ben has just started to drive, and has been told to keep his phone on 'do not disturb' and in the glove box when doing so. In a happy accident of timing, the UK government is supporting me with this, and has just passed a law which says that if you are caught using a mobile phone in the car within two years of passing your test, then you lose your license and have to retake your theory and practical exams once more.

For more experienced drivers, points and fines have doubled - but right now my son's safety is my primary concern and this additional motivation to keep focus on the road is welcome.

Anxiety

How do we measure general levels of anxiety? There are several tests available, but the most widely accepted is the Beck Anxiety Inventory (BAI) created by Dr. Aaron T. Beck.

There are 21 common symptoms of anxiety listed, in which you are asked to indicate how often such symptoms have bothered you during the last month. Possible symptoms include "Unable To Relax", "Hands Trembling" and "Difficulty in Breathing" the participant then selects from four possible answers:

Not At All (0)

Mildly but it didn't bother me much (1)

Moderately - it wasn't pleasant at times (2)

Severely - it bothered me a lot (3)

Why not take a moment and try the test for yourself, you can revisit this to measure your own levels of anxiety at any time - and it can be an illuminating method of understanding how various influences in your life affect your mental state. Note that this is not specific to anxiety caused by technology and the internet, that one will follow shortly.

Short Name	Score			
	0	1	2	3
Feeling hot				
Muscle numbness or tingling				
Feeling unable to relax				
Dizzy or light headed				
Feeling wobbly in the legs				
Feeling unsteady				
Heart racing or pounding				
Nervousness				
Choking feeling				
Trembling hands				
Unsteadiness				
Terror or fear				
Afraid of losing control				
Indigestion				
Flushed face				
Hot or cold sweats				
Feeling scared				
Having laborious breathing				
Feeling the fear of dying				
Feeling like the worst is happening				
Feeling faint				

If you scored less than seven, that's an indicator of a low anxiety level, although it can also illustrate a detachment from the world around you. Between eight and twenty-one gives you a moderate level that can be managed with relaxation techniques and behaviour change. If you score over twenty-two then you really need to take immediate action to address the underlying issues.

As we put more and more of our life online, we become increasingly obsessed with recording what we do - and then promoting the 'best bits' to others via social media.

This desire to record and share causes anxiety on a tech free day. But it also causes a great deal of anxiety on a day to day basis for many who believe that if you are not posting something positive about your life, you may be seen as worthless.

There is evidence that this anxiety can be exaggerated by exposure to social media in particular.

A study by psychologists Tara C. Marshall, Katharina Lefringhausen and Nelli Ferenczi at Brunel University linked certain kinds of Facebook activity to low self esteem and narcissistic behaviour. The research connected users who had completed an online survey measuring personality traits - extraversion, neuroticism, openness, agreeableness and conscientiousness, along with self-esteem and narcism and found that:

•People with low self-esteem more frequently post status updates about their current romantic partner.

- Narcissists more frequently updated their achievements, motivated by their need for attention and validation from the community. These updates also received a greater number of 'likes' and comments, indicating that narcissists' boasting may be reinforced buy the attention they crave.

- Narcissists also wrote more status updates about their diet and exercise routine, suggesting that they use Facebook to broadcast the effort they put into their physical appearance.

- Conscientiousness was associated with writing more updates about one's children.

- Extraverts more frequently update about their social activities

The challenge is that narcissistic behaviour can become even more attractive when others get the reward - I know several people that become depressed when they get no 'likes' for a post, and many others that delight in telling me how many 'likes' they get for things. Simply put, 'likes' trick your brain into thinking you have done something good.

Everyone likes positive affirmation, but a 'thumbs up' from others shouldn't be a driving factor in your life.

My children call this the pursuit of fake internet points, and one of the main violators of this are grandparents, newly arriving at Facebook and enraptured by the virtual adulation and information overload from hundreds of people that have been out of mind for decades. On the upside, it's certainly a partial cure for loneliness.

Returning to a post to check the number of likes and comments - regardless of platform causes a constant level of anxiety as does the fear of missing out (FOMO), and the complete focus on presenting an unrealistically positive, aspirational view of your own experience.

But anxiety does not stop there. Medically diagnosed 'stress behaviour' can occur after only a few minutes of separation from your mobile phone. Absurdly, this stress can be reduced by holding somebody else's mobile phone (you did read that right), just like the comfort blanket or teddy bear you may have had as a child.

In a study by the Department of Ethology, Eötvös Loránd University, Budapest in Hungary took 48 men and 94 women from the age of 18-26, removed half of their mobile phones and then asked them to sit in a room performing set activities on a laptop. During the breaks, those who had their phones taken away tended to hover around the cupboard where their phone was locked, fidget, touch their faces, scratch and experience accelerated heart rate.

This is why many people start to feel stressed when their phone runs out of battery or is mislaid - they are literally suffering from the same sort of separation anxiety as an infant denied human contact or their favourite comforter.

The authors of the report* created the Mobile Attachment Scale

(MAS) questionnaire reproduced here - the higher the score, the more likely you are to suffer from anxiety. You can assess your own level of attachment here.

On a scale of one to five, to what extent are the following statements characteristic of you? Where 1=Not at all characteristic of me, and 5=Very characteristic of me.

Item	Score
I regularly check my phone even if it does not ring.	☐
I feel bad when I leave my phone at home/ when it runs out of battery.	☐
My phone is within my reach even at night.	☐
If I left my phone at home, I would be willing to go home for it.	☐
When I sit down somewhere (e.g. in a cafe, a lecture, at a dining table, etc.), I put my phone at a visible place, within my	☐
I'm nervous if I cannot be reached on the phone.	☐
I'm nervous if I cannot get through to somebody immediately.	☐
If a close friend/ family member doesn't pick up the phone, I start to worry/ have a bad feeling.	☐
I prefer talking about awkward things on the phone rather than face to face.	☐
I prefer settling a dispute (with partner, family members, etc.) on the phone rather than face to face.	☐

*Veronika Konok, Dóra Gigler, Boróka Mária Bereczky, Ádám Miklósi

Score yourself for each of these, then calculate the average (divide by 10) to give yourself a MAS number. The higher the number, the more anxious you are likely to be should your phone be taken away from you, lost or destroyed.

Fitness bands and smart watches are becoming increasingly popular, the humble smart phone can also track activity - and there are distinct benefits to connecting yourself to one of these devices, one of our close friends lost 21 kg over the course of year using one - but I never saw him share progress on line, he was competing with himself.

If you like to share your runs or fitness statistics online, then how hard can it be to wait until Monday to do it? If you start to feel anxious about not doing it immediately, then the chances are you have a problem.

High levels of anxiety cause a number of negative effects to take place - from short terms effects such as an inability to concentrate, and headaches and fatigue to long term effects such damage to the hippocampus cells in the brain - affecting memory and learning. This is clearly not a state anybody should be in for any significant amount of time - and yet the increasing pressure of being connected 24/7 causes an increase in that very behaviour.

This anxiety extends in the most unexpected ways within our family too. Our fifteen year old son Gabriel is a Snapchat user, and one Sunday (with no mobile data available) started to beg me to turn the internet feed back on so he could add to his 'streak'.

For the uninitiated, a streak is when a picture gets sent (and reciprocated) by an individual or group - so if Gabriel sends a picture to his friend, and the friend responds - that's 1. The next day the process repeats, 2. And so on.

Several of the parents I know have children with streaks in excess of 500. That means that every day, for 500 days, they have sent at least one picture through Snapchat. Scary.

This of course drives addictive behaviour, and on this particular Sunday Gabriel got extremely anxious about reaching a streak of sixty. By pleading with me, he knew that I would find out that he'd been cheating the system on previous tech free days - and he knew there would be adverse consequences. But that didn't stop him.

It drove a very entertaining discussion with Ben (who does not use Snapchat), Gabe and myself about fake internet points, pointless behaviour, and the ways these companies hook people onto their platforms.

Withdrawal

"Fear is the memory of pain. Addiction is the memory of pleasure.
Freedom is beyond both."

Deepak Chopra

If you stop using the internet, even for a short amount of time, you are going to start suffering from withdrawal symptoms. You may not believe this to be so, but it is true. The extent of those withdrawal symptoms will be dependent on a number of factors - not just how long you use the web each day, but also what you use it for and when.

Think of it this way, when you do something pleasurable, your brain rewards you with dopamine in your mesolimbic pathway. When this happens you want to do more of whatever it is that caused it. Sometimes this is harmful, sometimes it is not - but it's a key part of your motivational system.

Your brain will adapt. Over time, increased levels of dopamine are normalised as neurons are desensitised. In order to gain the same 'reward', you need to do more (or more extreme) repeats of the pattern of behaviour you started with.

Recreational narcotics work by flooding the relevant pathways in the brain with greatly increased levels of dopamine, the pleasure gained from internet connectivity is a much more gradual build, although this does depend on exactly what you are using the internet for.

If you stop performing any behaviour that gives you pleasure, particularly one that you have been exposed to for a long period of time - then the absence of dopamine is going to lead to a progression of withdrawal symptoms that are well documented as the brain attempts to regulate the neurochemical system.

The longer you spend on the internet each day, your age, and the length of time you have been doing it will define the strength of your addiction. A strong enough addiction will result in more extreme withdrawal.

These will include (all of which we observed in ourselves as we reduced our tech consumption). Irritability, anxiety, physical tension, depression, change in appetite, change in mood, restlessness, insomnia, increased aggression/anger, strange dreams and craving for access.

These won't be too bad for the first few hours, but they will build, and if you decide to take a week off, you'll find that days two and three are the worst. Just like any drug based addiction, you're going to feel that 'need' for more for several months, or even years.

Which is why, in the second part of the book, there are guidelines to reduce consumption as painlessly as possible.

But be warned - withdrawal is a very real barrier to doing this, and it's very hard to decode seemingly rational statements with those driven by withdrawal.

Typical statement: "This is stupid, you're just trying to control me, it's normal to have access to the internet and my phone, shout, yell, bang door"

Translation: "My expected dopamine levels are down, I cannot get my fix so I'm going to have an epic teenage tantrum"

Memory

"Sometimes you will never know the value of a moment until it becomes a memory."

Theodor (Dr.) Seuss Geisel

Manfred Spitzer coined the phrase "Digital Dementia" in his 2012 book of the same name. Evidence suggests that using smart devices for prolonged periods of time damages short-term memory. When I was younger not only could I remember the phone numbers of all my friends, I needed to.

It was that or carry a Filofax around all day (remember them?).

Now our phones do this for us. But that's not the whole story - more and more people use their phones to record every critical juncture of the day - taking pictures of paintings, monuments, landmarks and particularly good cups of coffee.

When we head off to rock concerts, it's normal for us to see half the audience watching the stage through their phone screen. Madness.

This has been shown to cause lateralisation of brain function - forcing one hemisphere of the brain to become dominant at the expense of the other, lowering our ability to concentrate and connect abstract concepts, damaging memory and increasing the likelihood of depression.

By recording everything we do, we are rewiring our brains to diminish the importance of 'living in the moment' - this is known as cognitive offloading, and while it is easy to think of our internet connection and smart phones as 'external hard drives' for the brain - we simply do not work that way.

As with most things, balance is key - and in the case of memory we need a balanced 'big picture' and 'small detail' to properly be able to recall events and details in the future, and our ability to do this is governed by the level of attention we can devote to what is directly in front of us.

Short term memory feeds long term memory. The richer the experience, the more sights, sounds and physical feelings that you absorb, the greater the benefit to your long term recall of that particular moment in time - and it's within long term memory that your new experiences associate with past ones.

Spending even part of the 'moment' with head down, face buried in a device will diminish your memory.

When we are multi-tasking we cannot devote enough time to absorbing the detail and context of what is around us - which in turn leads to diminished recall of facts.

Thankfully, behaviour change can reverse these effects over time, a process that can be speeded up by focusing on more creative pursuits. Evidence suggests that learning a musical instrument can increase the size of the connecting nerves between our two brain hemispheres (the corpus callosum), improve verbal memory and literacy skills and even speed up stroke rehabilitation.

Two of our children are keen musicians, Jessica and Gabriel. The two least addicted to the internet, and least affected by our digital diet. I'm not at all sure this is a coincidence.

Summary

So there you have it.

Just like any tool, when used improperly the internet and associated technologies are dangerous. This should not come as a shock, but let me take a moment to summarise the challenges that using the internet is causing for you (and by extension, your family).

You are overloaded with information on a daily basis, which makes it difficult to think and hard to be productive - but because you're used to this you may well consider this to be a normal, inescapable part of life. Many people in our society are digitally obese, and you may be one of them.

Due to a need to belong to the tribe, a hunger in your brain caused by extensive prior usage, your natural curiosity and the human propensity to become addicted to pleasure you may be struggling to get a good nights sleep, interrelate with those around you and get enough exercise.

Trying to give up the internet or the technology you use is ridiculously impractical in the modern world, and even though you know you need to restrict your consumption and diet - you are going to have a tough time doing it - you'll get anxious, the lack of distraction will exaggerate your withdrawal symptoms and your mind will focus on the lack of dopamine as a method of forcing you back to your device.

On top of all that, your family may either celebrate or rebel against this idea in equal measure. Half of the people you know think you're crazy for trying, the other half will secretly admire you for having a go - but they'll also expect you to fail.

Having read this far, you know that if you manage to go on a digital diet you're going to be rewarded by more time together, better connections to those around you, a reduced waistline, better memory, greater productivity, greater fitness and a renewed appreciation for the world around you.

It may take a few months, but trust me, the effort will be worth it.

The next part of the book is all about my family, and our experiences breaking the habit.

Part 2: Our Story

"That period of time was nostalgic, I think that people have such affection for Friends because there was something about a time when our faces weren't shoved into cell phones and we weren't checking Facebooks and Instagrams, and we were in a room or a coffee shop together and we were talking. Having a conversation. We've lost that." - Jennifer Aniston

Our Story

Once upon a time, before we had children, my Wife and I (along with three friends) hopped on a plane to Boston, drove north and spent a happy few days snowmobiling in northern New Hampshire. We rented a log cabin that had a little wood burning stove, a radio and nothing else.

Of course, this was before the internet had truly taken hold - but the memory of the mental peace and quiet often serves as a reminder of how things could be for us. For some of our friends it's the beach, or the pool, or skiing, or even fishing - whatever your 'peaceful' image is I can almost guarantee it doesn't involve technology - or at least an internet connection.

One Sunday morning three years ago, it dawned on me that we were as far as humanly possible from our log cabin. Conversation had been lost, but the house was far from silent.

In the living room, arguments were breaking out over which TV show to watch, upstairs the Wii was causing a fight for some reason and I had my phone out at the breakfast table, checking the news because Caroline was watching a breakfast show on the kitchen iMac.

In a way that perhaps only parents can understand, I had a 'moment' - failing to resolve the arguments around me (which were disturbing my own gadget enjoyment) I switched it all off. Everything - the TV, the gaming, the router - and announced that the day was going to be spent without the gadgets.

This was received with widespread approval from the whole family.

Or not. In fact emphatically, cataclysmically not.

The whole day was spent filled with resentment and upset. Everyone was irritable, we all got on each others nerves. Sunday lunch was the only break from the discontent, as they all sat around and complained about me - at least that was a uniting moment.

That night, Caroline and I reflected on all this and she (as the least technically tethered in the family) recognised our challenge for what it was. An addiction.

I've spoken to a lot of people during the last few years about our experiences, and I can assure you that admitting this is the hardest thing. The biggest blockage to doing something about it.

So, for the sake of solidarity let me tell you that I am addicted to the technology we have and in particular the internet.

"My name is Mark Ellis and I am an internet addict"

I don't like being out of control, and I don't like the thought of addiction - and I positively hate the idea that my children could be ensnared by it.

So our reaction to our appalling first day was not to give up, or blame me for singular irrational behaviour - it was to carry on with more of the same. But a word of warning - it get's harder before it get's easier.

As I said in the introduction, one thing this book isn't about is how to be a parent - families are all different, and everyone has their own way of doing things. But for the sake of context I asked the children to rate my Wife and I on a scale of 1 to 10 in 'strictness' compared to their friends parents with the following question:

"On a scale of one to ten, where one is 'we let you do whatever you like' and ten is 'we control every aspect of your life' where would you score us?

Think about your friends, and where you think they might score before you answer.

We scored

7.6

Ouch. We think we're around a 5 - so draw your own conclusions from this. What I will say is that we expect the children to do some jobs around the house, be polite to each other and not fight (verbally or physically). I absolutely want to be friends with them, but my first priority is to be a parent.

We never set out to cancel technology in the house - it happened because my Wife and I felt it was the best thing we could do for our family - and I'm long overdue in introducing you, the reader, to the people I share my home with.

Mark

Me first. I'm a semi-reformed technoholic, with a love for data, and an even greater love for people - in particular how well they fit in their jobs, how happy they are at work, and whether their work/ life balance is working out well. My day job sees me working with lots of different companies who are trying to become more productive by building the right culture for their employees.

I've worked all over the world, I have a fancy card from an airline with 1 million miles stamped on the corner which I used to be proud of...... I am absolutely reliant on technology to stay in touch with my family, friends and business contacts - and my computer is a critical business tool.

I love my job. I get to indulge my passion and my skills and for the most part (hopefully) make others happier. Some of the people I know from the companies I work with will make guest appearances later on, because some of the lessons we've learned as a family have corporate applications.

Caroline

My beautiful, amazingly talented and tolerant Wife. We've been married for over twenty years and I still have no idea what I did to get so lucky, or how she puts up with me.

When our first child arrived she gave up her job at a top London graphic design agency to look after him, and after seventeen years and three more children she now has her own graphic design practice - splitting her time between charitable and corporate work.

She is the creative half of our relationship - pens, pencils, paper and models - and only in the last few years have computers and smart phones entered her life.

Ben

The eldest, he's seventeen years old at the time of writing this book - and in the middle of his sixth form year. Since the age of eight he's been obsessed with becoming a marine biologist - and he's taking Physics, Chemistry and Biology at A' level. He managed to find himself a place in a Marine Biology Institute in Norway to do his work experience, and is also crack shot with a bow and arrow (he spent this summer teaching children the craft at Warwick Castle) after winning a national Scout archery competition.

He's totally and utterly obsessed with Minecraft, Imgur and a bunch of other things that you may or may or may not have heard of.

Gabriel

Fifteen years old, with a gift for music. He writes songs, is rarely seen without a guitar of some sort in his hand and loves bands and artists ranging from McBusted to AC/DC via Dolly Parton and Brad Paisley. He despises One Direction with a passion that borders on the unhealthy.

He's also borderline dyslexic, and has worked very hard to rise through the streams at school. He's got no clue what he wants to do outside playing his guitar and singing - but he enjoys being in school plays, school choir, cooking and art.

Jessica

Thirteen years old, just started secondary school and pretty much loves all things pink. She's a sports nut - volunteering for all things in school despite being one of the smallest in the year. In the first week of her new school she was the only girl on the football (soccer) team - won the cross country running competition, and played hockey and netball too.

She's very creative, into her drawing, painting and piano - and she's a dab hand at biscuit making too. She's also a bit of maths geek like her eldest brother.

Noah

Seven years old. Definitely the happiest of the bunch, because he gets constant attention from his siblings (and Mum & Dad). Absolutely excellent at pretending to be a super hero or a baby animal, he has been exposed to far too many unsuitable films involving gods with hammers and men in iron suits beating up bad guys.

Where is he academically? Despite all government attempts to the contrary, we really couldn't care less - he seems bright enough, but we'd rather he spends time playing rather than starting on quantum physics just yet.

So that's us - and we have a bunch of technology to tempt us - the elder three children have hand-me-down smartphones, we all have a laptop or a desktop computer (excepting the youngest) and then there's the games console, the streaming TV boxes and a couple of tablets for good measure.

Gabriel actually saved for his own iPad, and tended to take offence at having it controlled, but as we pay for the electricity, food and internet subscription we believe we have that right to do this.

Day One

Which brings us back to day one. In retrospect it was inevitable what happened. The 'decision' to stop the internet was taken at around 10am - which left a giant hole in the day for all of us (except my Wife). I wasn't thinking straight, and naively thought of it as a 'punishment' and inflicted it as such.

To the rest of the family I simply "took their toys away", and I neglected to consider the effect avoiding wi-fi would have on me too. I couldn't be hypocritical and dive back in through my phone data plan - but we had no plans for the day.

As the router was gone, and there was no internet flowing into the house, the control aspect was easy. Phones were placed in the kitchen (which is the centre of our home), and so 'sneaking on' wasn't a challenge - but boredom soon set in.

Our day was a fractious affair - I made the mistake of getting Monopoly out of the cupboard thinking that would be a 'cool' thing to do, but that just created more arguments and resentment. At one point we decided to go for a walk, but then couldn't decide where to go.

After about an hour, the children picked up Nerf guns and headed outside to shoot at each other for a while. That did seem to help - and they returned in a much better mood for Sunday lunch.

More arguments ensued afterwards, the idea of watching only what was on the TV seemed to cause even more challenges (which teenager doesn't love a Sunday night BBC period drama?) and everyone headed to bed a little earlier than normal.

To be honest, day one was easy compared to the next few weeks - the unexpected nature of the tech free event, and the lack of knowledge that this could continue potentially made things a little smoother.

I recognised the siren song of the technology for the addiction it was, and I worried that the children were going to get hooked too. Caroline and I made the decision that we were going to do something about it, and we've kept one day tech free ever since. For us it's "Tech Free Sunday", for some friends of ours its 'Wi-fi free Wednesday" - whichever day you choose, I'm sure you'll come up with your own catchy title.

Breaking In

Here's a suggestion for you. Going cold turkey is not for everyone. Retrospectively we would have started the ball rolling gently with daily mandated 'breaks' in our wi-fi and screen use.

We do this now and we did this from the Monday after day one. Here are our two golden rules:

No phones or tablets at the dinner table. Ever. No devices when eating. Possible pitfalls here include "I use my phone as a remote for the music", or "I'm expecting a call". Don't listen and don't make an exception to this one. Keep them out of pockets, out of sight, and even out of the room if possible. This starts to get the brain used to the absence of something it has learned to believe is necessary for survival.

Put the tech away at some point in the evening. Given the ages of our children, and the life we have our 'curfew' is either 7pm or 8pm depending on circumstance. Again, this demonstrates that not having the technology to hand is **OK**. Possible objections here also include "I'm expecting a call", or "we can all watch YouTube together", or even - "I need the internet to do my homework" (more on that one later).

You'll find that rather than stopping for the day, limiting the use as a first step will get the idea of 'restraint' into everyone's head.

Think of trying to lose weight - if you are used to eating 4000 calories a day, and suddenly drop to 1000 calories a day your body will react poorly to that. Not least because physically your stomach is of a size to accommodate much more food than you are providing it, and it's going to scream "HUNGRY" at you all day.

In the same way, a steady reduction of tech at certain times allows your brain to accept the idea that it's not critical for human survival.

Technical Exceptions

The breaking in period allows you to realise that sometimes exceptions need to be made. These can be different for everyone - but experience tells us that they generally fall into three distinct groups - Exceptions, Grey Areas and Nevers.

Exceptions

Cameras

Once upon a time you stood before a man with a tray of flash powder, then came the Brownie, pocket sized cameras, instant Polaroid cameras then the digital cameras that really changed the way we see the world once more. The last evolutionary jump drew a line with professional SLR camera's on one side of the divide and smartphone cameras on the other.

Practically speaking, in social events we all like to have memories. Sometimes unexpectedly amazing things happen and we want to record them - a sunset, a wonderful meal, herds of wildebeest sweeping majestically across the plains, or just a cute picture of one of the children.

Whatever the reason, not having the ability to use a camera is just dumb and unrealistic. You can argue that they are distractions too - but in our world that's simply not going to happen. But there are some limits.

Don't share the picture, comment on it, edit it (I'm thinking Instagram here). You can do that tomorrow - this comes under the heading of delaying gratification. If that photo still seems amazing in the morning, feel free to share it, edit it and fiddle with it all you like.

Likewise, unless you're a food critic, you don't need to take a picture of everything you consume - I used to laugh at people taking pictures of their dinner, until I found myself doing the same in a coffee shop. Doh.

Unless you're a photo journalist or a reporter you don't need to record everything and although you can take hundreds of digital pictures, every day it doesn't mean you have to.

So using a gadget as a camera is OK for us, and it may well be for you too.

Sport

Swimmers, runners, triathletes, cyclists - you name it, there's an app for that. Many of us use the apps to record times, distances and routes - and it makes no sense to stop doing that.

If I look through the apps on my phone, I've got one for recording swim times during meets and another that we use for tracking our cycle routes and competing with our friends. It would be hard to argue that these do not benefit our health and wellbeing, but the trick is not to 'share' what you're doing while your curfew is going.

Another benefit of spending time exercising as a family (for example cycling to the pub) is that the more you ride, the more you want to ride. The children like spending the whole day out if the weather is good, but that raises another challenge if you decide to explore new places.

Think about it - as your distance increases, so does the challenge of finding your way, and instinct now has us reaching for the phone, bringing up a map, and working out a route - but I can assure you that you'll have a lot more fun buying an Ordinance Survey map for an area and poring over it with the family before you head out. Apart from the educational benefit you can see a lot more - hills, pubs, bridleways etc. are all plainly visible - as are landmarks that you wouldn't normally notice using your phone.

Homework

This is all about judgement, common sense and compromise. In the early days of our 'experiment' Ben soon worked out that homework could be his free pass to the web.

Practical reality is that students need access to the web. We can argue about the ethics of this, and the exclusion of the poorest in society - but just like the Luddites, we need to accept that homework and internet access are joined at the hip.

We'll dig into this in much more detail - but effectively homework needs to be done earlier rather than later. Otherwise great fun can be had internet gaming, surfing the web and Skyping friends until 7pm, and then telling your parents that you need the web for homework.

There are exceptions - deadlines, tough assignments, exam revision - every schedule is different, but be careful of changing priorities to get the 'pass' for an extension of web time.

Grey Areas

Diets

If you are dieting and recording your food intake (or looking up calories) using an app - then whether you use your phone in curfew time is up to you. Some people I know are content to write down their consumption and type it in the following day - some genuinely don't know the calories without looking them up.

Our advice and experience would say this is a bad thing - becoming too obsessed with recording progress leads further down the addiction route.

Satnav

I have an in car satnav system, but it doesn't remotely compare the amazing ability of the one that sits on my phone. Clearly the phone needs to be secured in the car (ideally in the hands of a passenger), and with all other alerts turned off (see later chapter). This is the most efficient way to get me and my family from point A to point B. The app we use also dynamically reroutes for fuel efficiency and traffic flow - so we feel that it's a safe and responsible use of technology during curfew.

Phones

We take a phone with us when we go out, in case anyone needs to get in touch with us and for emergency use (especially when we go out cycling). Honestly, I'd rather not - but the practicality of life necessitates it. The funny thing is that people rarely call - there are so many other forms of communication that the actual 'speaking to someone' thing is typically used only in extreme circumstances, and as the phone is set to 'do not disturb' it quickly becomes forgotten.

Movie/TV Streaming

Once upon a time TV came through the aerial on the roof, then through a cable or a satellite dish, and now through the phone line too in the form of Netflix, Amazon Prime and other on-demand catch up services. After some debate, we decided that these would be allowed if, and only if, three or more people wanted to watch something.

That might seem daft, but in the absence of instant gratification from one source, the natural tendency for our children was to find a series to binge watch - and these were typically low grade entertainment with hundreds of episodes. The 'group' watching mentality stops this from happening as it's rare to find something that everyone wants to watch in this category.

Nevers

Trackers

I used to feel sorry for animals that were tranquillised and then tagged, tracked and monitored. One of my favourite Gary Larson cartoons illustrated this as male bear arrives home, ear tagged, tracking collar fitted and tattooed with "No. 8" to find the lady bear saying "Late again! This better be good!" Now we do it to ourselves. If not through the phone, then through smart bracelets of one sort or another.

I love my Fitbit, it helps keep me moving, and I love the way I can compete with my friends in various challenges. I like keeping an eye on my heart rate.

After 7, and on Sunday's it still takes some self-control not to open the app and check progress. But that's worth doing - because the moment you glance at the phone, you may see an alert you need to respond too. Your fitness gadget will carry on regardless, and will sync on Monday morning just fine.

Skype/Facetime

We used to treat this one as an exception, but the reality is that it offers up too much temptation to stray. We still have a 'land line' phone, and we use that on a Sunday. All our friends know this, so it's no big deal. But the minute you grab a device during curfew - your going to test your self control.

"Find It" Apps

Our phones are full of these - I need a coffee, where can I find one? I need to find the nearest sandwich shop. I need to seek out my favourite brand of organic sushi. And so it goes on. There is no need for these - in a world where people are starving, being fundamentally attached to a particular food, drink or retail brand is probably not healthy. We can certainly manage a day off.

One day in February we emerged from the British Museum, having taken three of the children to see some of the exhibits (Noah in particular wanted to be a Pharaoh) we emerged into the cold and damp anxious to find some food - the coffee and cake were good in the museum, but McDonalds was the request from the small people.

Normally, I'd flick open the finder app on my phone and search......but of course it was a Sunday. What to do? Luckily there was a human being nearby, so I asked him if he knew where the nearest McDonalds was and five minutes later we were sitting in the warmth.

Email

Yes, email has to be in the mix. A mentor of mine who had previously worked at Motorola told me over a decade ago never to let work email follow me home. I wish I had listened better - but that is wisdom beyond measure.

Some companies have policies in place to prevent this from happening, but for the most part, we're expected to be plugged into email 24x7 - and it's not fair or appropriate. Can you really, hand on heart, tell me that you cannot live without your email for the day?

When you go on holiday, take a flight or stay in hospital do you find that the world has stopped turning in your absence? Of course not.

(Although to my horror, on a recent flight to the US, the internet was available on board - this is quiet relax and work time for me, and the thought that I could be bothered at 30,000 feet distressed me beyond measure.)

A friend recently told me that he never looks at email unless he has time to respond, otherwise he's doubling his workload and stressing about responding. This struck me as a great additional discipline.

Out of office messages are perfectly acceptable, and we all use them. The people who know me can always get in touch with a phone call if it's urgent so stop making excuses and switch off your email during curfew.

Text

Texting is a major influence on hyper-vigilance - because of the ease and cost of doing so. Not only are text messages becoming 'richer', and more able to contain pictures, animations and entertainment - but they are offered free by most phone companies as they take up so little network space. They create alerts as they come in, and we have all become accustomed to instant replies.

I feel myself getting upset when someone doesn't respond to one of my text messages, and I feel the desire to grab and respond when my phone goes off on our tech free days or after 7pm. Unlike most of the things on this list, texts can come via the cellular network or the internet, so this needs careful management.

One Sunday, I glanced up from the table to see Caroline reaching for her phone on the other side of the kitchen - she pushed the 'on' button, and glanced down at the screen. Within 30 seconds she was hunched over it tapping away.

As is customary for any of us I called out "What are you doing?! No tech!"

"It's Isabel asking if Jessica would like to come round to their house after Church"

"But we're going to Church and you'll see Isabel there"

"Yes, but she sent a text, it would be rude to ignore it"

"If you hadn't looked, you wouldn't have know about it"

This is a perfect example of why we do it. Thirty minutes after this exchange we were in Church, Caroline and Isabel would have had a chat, and Jessica would have headed off to her friends house. Tech unnecessary.

Over coffee after the service, we were all talking about this, and although this is a complication when interacting with others - the expectation that a response will be forthcoming as soon as you send a text (and to a lesser extent email), nobody is likely to take offence - and it's a great opportunity to talk about the how and why we're dropping tech for the day.

Managing Expectations

Not yours, but those of others. The breaking in period is a great time to deal with this, and get a feeling for how difficult it's going to be.

In the first half of the book we talked about FOMO - the fear of missing out. This is not a problem just within the social media space, but also between friends. One of the biggest challenges for us is that we DO miss out.

It's far less frequent than it used to be, but at the start of our journey we missed out on all kinds of things because we 'hadn't seen the message'. This could be a text inviting us round to friends, or a cinema trip - or almost anything. We missed out on concert tickets from sick friends.

But that's life. None of us should expect to see, control and be part of everything that goes on around us.

The greater challenge is getting the message across to friends that you really cannot be reached this way when the technology is turned off. It's amusing to us when we constantly remind people that we do actually have a phone - and it works, and we answer it.

A few years ago, we removed the wireless phones, and replaced them with old fashioned ones - one in my study, and one in the kitchen. They look nicer, and at the time meant that conversations happened in public - so it suited our needs.

They are also loud - actual bells ring during a call, and they are tough to ignore. We'll also answer our cellphones if they ring. As mentioned in the 'exceptions' section, typically either Caroline or I will have ours with us, even if we don't intend to use it.

We did not make any grand announcement that we were giving up technology for one day a week, or that we don't have it in the evenings. We just stopped, and then apologised the following day and explained why we hadn't responded sooner.

Nobody cares.

That's the cold hard truth - although we all have these expectations of being constantly on call, we have yet to find somebody who is offended by our behaviour, and we've not missed any life changing events because of it.

A Personal Experiment

Here are four quick things for you try before you start experimenting on your family - you may find them easy or hard, but having some personal experience of doing this is going to help when you try and impose a new regime on all the addicts around you.

1. Stop taking devices to the bedroom. Turn them off, leave them downstairs and don't look at them within half an hour of going to bed. This will improve the production of melatonin in your brain and help you get to sleep - but you are likely to feel some anxiety at doing so. Remember this feeling. Oh - and according to multiple studies this will certainly improve your sex life.

2. Don't pick up your phone until 30 minutes after you get out of bed in the morning. Various studies show that between 80% and 90% of people check their phones within 5 minutes of waking up - this fuels all the behaviours we are trying to avoid.

3. Turn off alerts on your phone for one day. You will then have to make a conscious effort to check them - regardless of social media platform, email, messages. This will give you an idea of how many times you actually do this.

4. Do not under any circumstance bring your smartphone to the table/sofa/restaurant when you eat. Doing so limits social

connection, reduces the body's natural enjoyment of food and company and builds new pathways in the brain connecting pleasure from eating to internet access.

If you cannot do any of these things, and you find yourself making excuses - then you have a serious addiction, and the next steps are going to be very tough for you. If you had no problem doing any of this, then you're going to have to learn to be empathetic with your family when you start the process of withdrawal.

Step 1 - Turn It Off

I'm going to assume (as you've got this far) that you are going to at least try and set some limits on the information flow into your home. Breaking-in time is a wonderful way of working out where the boundaries are and how to handle them.

This is going to sound bad, but honestly physically turning off the box that brings the internet into your home is the best (and simplest) way to start your journey.

There are two ways data flows into your home, the first is through a magic box called a router. This is the thing that hangs off your phone line and broadcasts the internet around your home.

It's the easiest thing in the world to control this, as it will certainly have an off switch, either at the wall, or on the box itself. Go and turn it off. Just do it. Nothing bad will happen.

(The other way data flows in is through cellular data and we'll look at that in the next chapter.)

This is not the route we took at first. I'm a bit of a geek (and if you are too, then this method may work) - so I gathered all the IP addresses from the devices in the house, opened up the security settings on the router, and set time limits on every device.

It's actually not that complicated. On the up side of this, it does mean that when you're not in the house, the curfew happens automatically - you can also leave a few devices tethered (so you can use Netflix in the lounge, but none of the computers will work.

On the downside, some providers allow 'hot spots' in your home that you cannot control. This is to allow visitors or passers by to quickly hop onto data without bothering you. We found that the children's friends would hand out their passwords to allow them to bypass the controls we had in place.

Devious creatures, kids (although I'm always secretly proud when they find a way around things that I hadn't thought of). We started using the same provider for their phone SIM card, and fixed the problem that way as controls 'extended' across our entire family account.

We have a slightly more complicated system in our house - we have two routers, one that brings the web in from the outside world, and then another one that connects all our computers and infrastructure together.

Router one (for us) is our trusty British Telecom (BT) one. Router two is an Apple Airport Extreme. Why is this important? Well, we have a media server - a computer full of music, films and photos that we access from devices all over the house. Router one gets turned off, and router two still manages all our internal flow.

Regardless - my advice is to unplug the router and put it in a drawer if you have to. On one memorable occasion, I actually hid it in my bag and accidentally took it with me the next day. I was not popular.

The world will not stop turning. So tonight, turn off your router at 7pm - and turn it back on when you get up in the morning.

...Or Don't Turn It Off

Of course turning the internet router off doesn't stop data coming in. Not any more - we can now access the web through our phones - in fact I've been known to tether my laptop to my phone to improve my bandwidth.

This is where things get a little more difficult. We decided on a two step process with this one.

Find an area (downstairs) that's central and visible, with access to a power socket or two. When curfew rolls around, ask everyone to leave their phones and tablets in plain sight, and plug them in. It may be that you need to buy another gadget that lets you charge multiple devices at once, but it's worth it.

We used to just have a nice box to put everything in, but it's tougher to charge things in there, and it's less obvious when one of the family 'forgets' about the 7pm limit.

The second step was a financial one too - we limited the monthly data plans on the children's phones to 500mb. More than enough for most things, but definitely enough to need wi-fi whenever it's available to ensure the allowance lasts a full month.

It took three months before any of them broke the data limit, they received a text, I paid a little more that month, and they got a clearer education into what their habits cost.

Interestingly we tracked the problem back to a power cut when their phones automatically switched to the cell network and consumed their entire allowance in a matter of hours.

A few months after that incident, another broke the data limit - and significantly. They had ignored multiple texts from the provider about it, and run up over £80 worth of additional data surfing. In this instance the router wasn't reaching far enough and the phone was lapsing back onto cell data - despite my best efforts at explaining how to manage this, clearly I hadn't done a good enough job.

Since that time, I've managed to find a way to cap their data so they cannot approve their own extensions - which was simple and easy to do.

If you're a novice at this yourself, here's a rough guide:

Wi-fi networks are freely available almost everywhere. When you're at home you almost certainly attach you devices to an internet router or hub and surf happily without touching your data allowance. This costs you absolutely nothing additional on your phone plan.

Out in the world, you need to consume GPRS, 3G, 4G or even 5G data from the cellphone towers - this costs money, and as there are so many people using them, this is the single most expensive element of your monthly plan. Exceed the data allowance within the plan, and the costs start increasing fast.

The phone manufacturers and the cell phone companies are not great with allowing the tracking of consumption. Most phones have a section in the settings that allows usage to be viewed, but you have to remember to reset it at the right time each month and check it regularly. Alternatively you can get on their web sites and track things that way, or download an app to do it.

Most importantly, it's critical to note the symbols at the top of the phone - see the little 'fan' symbol and wi-fi is being used - anything else and you're in trouble. Data is not air, it is not free - and explaining all of this helps children understand the technology, the risks and the cost of accessing the web from different locations.

Even now, we still slip - I recently went back to turning off the router, and four days later all the children ran out of data. Suspicious eh? They had been sneaking phones upstairs and getting online, without realising they were using their data allowance.

The lesson was learned.

Reflection

This is your time to reflect - the point in this detox process to be honest with yourself about the family rankings for internet addiction. For us it was:

1 Mark

2 Ben

3 Noah

4 Gabriel

5 Jessica

6 Caroline

These 'rankings' come from common sense, rather than extensive discussion, and it's going to tell you how hard it's going to be to make any of this work. If you are at the bottom of this list, then it's going to be tougher than it was for me - because you're going to have a hard time accepting that this is a problem.

If you are too near the top, then you run the risk of becoming an irrational dictator as you battle your own addiction, the responsibility of being a parent, and the task of bringing everyone on the journey with you.

The parents I know who have 'given up' on this idea generally don't fully grasp that it's possible to be addicted. They know something is wrong, but without suffering themselves it seems harder to drag their family through it. Without feeling something of the withdrawal symptoms from the first half of the book - motivation to make the change seems lower.

If this is you, and placing the curfew made no difference to you personally, do not fall into the trap.

If it made no difference then why not stick with it a bit longer? It's not an inconvenience for you after all. But do watch those around you carefully, and take note of any changes.

No matter where you are in the ranking of addiction, you should notice two things afterwards - It shouldn't have been too tough, and you may have more self awareness of the things you are compelled to do with your devices.

Among other things, I miss the ability to look at the weather forecast.

The weather. Yes, I'm British. There is no time in my day that I don't want to assess the weather - especially now we're spending more time on days out with the family. The phone is great for this - but we've learned two lessons, weather is still on the TV every 30 minutes or so, and coats repel rainwater. We've also learned that our habits don't really change regardless of what the weather is like - it's not as if a cold wet day will suddenly become dry, hot and sunny.

Gabriel stuck his head around the study door a moment ago and I asked him what he misses the most. He said "It doesn't really bother me". I know he loves to watch music videos on YouTube, and when I pushed him on that he shrugged his shoulders and said "I just wait until tomorrow, it's no big deal".

I love the answer, but back when this started that wasn't the case with any of us.

It may help to make a list of the things you've missed, so you can look back on them, or share them with your friends to laugh at.

This is the time to stop taking the tech to the bedroom too. You can address those sleep issues a lot easier at this moment than at any other. Think of it this way - if you stopped with the gadgets at 7pm, then by the time you head to bed your melatonin levels should be building naturally. It may take a few weeks to properly resolve, but resisting the urge for one last screen glance will help you get a much better nights sleep.

Ironically, if you want to test this for yourself, and you have a Fitbit (I do like to experiment on myself and my family) - you can check your sleep pattern the following morning. After a week or so you should notice less disturbance, a slightly lower heart rate and fewer times 'awake'. Just don't check it on your tech free day!

What was that? You need to take your phone upstairs because you use it as an alarm clock, and you charge it at your bedside. These are the two most popular excuses - I've heard many more, from the "what if someone calls" to "my garage smoke alarm sends alerts to it". None of these are good excuses.

Move the charge cable downstairs, and buy a cheap alarm clock. If you're anything like us, you probably have one somewhere anyhow - and if not then Amazon have 817 alarm clock options under the £5 price boundary.

And remember, you're trying to avoid entering a state of hyper-vigilance when you're trying to sleep. It's probably going to help to turn off the phone too - you can put it to airline mode if you wish, but physically turning it off helps delay any urges you may have to cheat, and sends a message to your subconscious that it WILL NOT disturb you.

I had a conversation with one of my friends about this, he's convinced that it doesn't apply to him - he has the phone in airline mode when he goes to bed, he likes to look at the news when he wakes up (although he says that he isn't compelled too as the first thing he does). So he doesn't need to do it.

He might be right.

Or it's a blindspot - if you find the idea of leaving your phone in another room something you feel is not for you, then you're not being rational. Read this chapter, and the one on hyper-vigilance again, and stop making excuses. What's the big deal? If you do it for a week and notice no difference you've lost nothing.

Now is the perfect time to make a list. On a piece of paper (or here in the margin), scribble down the things you think you'll miss about not having access to the internet. After one evening write down any others that you were not expecting. You may surprise yourself with how compulsive you really are.

One of the big things that I miss is the ability to look at movie casts while the movie is on. Now I've written that down, it seems even more crazy - but nonetheless....I love films, and I have a pretty good knowledge of them - the old 'seven degrees of separation' game is one of my favourites (younger readers may have to look that up).

Yet I find myself tapping **IMDB** every time a movie is on, and cross referencing the cast to see what else I recognise them from. Never mind that I'm missing the film, withdrawing from the rest of the family, and off in my own little world (not to mention disturbing their viewing) - I'm indulging my need for instant gratification.

REFLECTION

What we discovered is that if it is really, really critical to know which movie that actor was in - we will remember to search for the answer in the morning.

This (as you might imagine) does not happen often.

Fringe Benefits

Let's assume that you've spent a few days with the 7pm curfew in place at this point. What you've learned is that you can actually live without your technical connection for a few hours every night.

But this isn't just about you, it's about the rest of the family too. We're all capable of making our own decisions, but somehow you've got to convince everyone to come on the journey with you.

Diets are tough, trying to lose weight is difficult - in order to do so, you need to change your habits, enjoy the exercise and live with the short term discomfort of being hungry. You also need to bear in mind that eating is addictive, and most diets fail as people give into compulsion and return to prior behaviour.

BUT - a food diet gives you visible benefit, your waistline reduces, your appearance improves, your breathing gets easier. An internet diet has less visible benefits, which is why some people refer to it as a detox.

Although most of the change goes on inside the brain, there are also many physical benefits that we overlooked when we began this experiment. For the most part, our tech keeps us sedentary - inside or sat down - and despite the future promise of spectacles carrying the web to our retinas, right now the biggest exception to this is Pokemon Go, which is getting a chapter all of it's own.

Aside from chasing virtual creatures with a phone in your hand, we noticed a massive shift in our families exercise habits. I'm not going to pretend we were ever a bunch of sofa dwelling potato chip eaters, but summer evenings are certainly more likely to see us outside and walking these days than inside and sat down.

One simple benefit was that the children started to join us more for dog walks - even Ben, who quite naturally at his age doesn't want to hang around with us all as much as he used to. With no internet, given the choice between sitting down and watching TV or reading a book or going for a walk - the exercise seems to become more appealing.

We also found that our trampoline was being used more - it turns out that it's a lot more fun to jump about in the sunshine than sit inside on a games console - who knew?

Taking the whole day off brings a lot more benefit, but I'd still advise you to hold off on taking that leap until you've spent at least two weeks in phase one, with the evening curfew.

Oh - one more thing, Jessica found a loophole in our system, and started getting up at 5am to binge on TV streaming before her brothers got up.

It also poses a challenge for our diet - we had an issue with Jessica getting up early in the morning and heading downstairs to binge watch streamed kids TV - the same stuff as she could watch in the early evening, but she just wasn't getting enough of it. At one point she was downstairs at 5:30am.

We also found the boys jumping out of bed and leaping to their computers and phones for the first few months.

The simple solution for us was to end our 'curfew' at 7am. The children get more sleep, have better levels of concentration in school, and are generally less grumpy.

Well, That Was Fun

You may have enjoyed doing something different. It's like switching to a fad diet, where you can make yourself feel great by realising you can exercise some self control. Given you have proved to yourself that you can do it, this is the moment where you're most likely to give up. Especially if you didn't notice a really big difference.

This is because all you have done is dealt with 'Delayed Gratification.' You've managed to begin teaching your brain that you can wait a short amount of time before it get's the hit it needs. This is a great start, but it's not truly dealing with the addiction.

But you've also shown yourself and your family that they can live without the web for short space of time, and when you take the next step this is really going to help avoid the withdrawal cataclysm that we observed in our home.

Of course, your family could have had a meltdown at the idea of a few hours off. In which case you very definitely know you have a problem. Some good friends of ours tried a curfew on a Wednesday night, and their daughter went into meltdown because she couldn't join a snapchat conversation.

Let's look at a few reasons why you might not want to move on to a full day off.

The first one is easy - you (like me) may not feel you can do it. I'm stubborn enough to test myself on this, and telling me I cannot do something is a guaranteed way to make me try; although if you're at the top of the addiction list you're going to find a million and one different excuses for why you don't want to do it though.

But there are lots of others reasons that I've heard.

It makes me smile when I talk through our family experiences and they tell me that it sounds fantastic, and they wish they could do it, but they can't because.....

Here are some of the reasons I've been given. And they are all terrible ones, and evidence of denial. That was mean and judgemental, but really, take a look for yourself and make up your own mind:

I'd love to do it, but my kids would have meltdown

I would still need to have access to my email

We've got this under control, I worry about the kids
sometimes, but I'm not addicted

It's just progress, you cannot stand in the way of it

There is no way my daughter would let me do it

My kids would literally leave home

If I stopped them at home, they'd find somewhere else to get
online

I'm just not technical enough to do this, my kids know
better than I do

I would rather educate them about this, than block them

I think our friends would admire the effort, but the kids
friends would think they were weird

There is just no way we could do this

You may as well just say - "I am slave to the internet and my
devices, and I don't care if my children are too."

Change is hard, but this is a change you need to make - and the best way to do that is to talk through all the reasons why you are doing it with the family.

They may not agree. You may not agree. But you'll never know until you try.

Step 2 - A Day Off

This is a big step. You might think it's not, and doing it for one day is not actually going to be that big a deal. In just the same way as trialling a curfew was easy.

But you are aiming to create a behaviour change, and although the evenings off help with this - the big ticket item is taking a whole day.

To make a new habit stick properly, you need to evidence to yourself that you can do it, find it enjoyable and prefer it to the alternative. This is what the diet industry call a lifestyle change - and it's exactly the same thing here. Let's imagine for a moment that you have an alcoholic drink every day - you don't get drunk and you're not an alcoholic. It's just something you enjoy.

Could you delay having a drink until 9pm? Of course you could. If you cannot, then you may well be an alcoholic. You are simply delaying your desire for that glass of wine, or beer - and it's easy because you know you'll get it shortly. Taking a day off is a bit tougher - especially if your friends or your partner are not joining you in your abstinence.

But there are studies that show taking a liver holiday is a really good idea - and this can be measured by chemicals in the bloodstream. Taking a internet holiday won't benefit your liver -

but it is going to benefit your brain.

There's another side effect of a 'liver holiday' - a reduction in the desire to have another drink. Effectively it makes it easier to resist the urge to have that glass of wine with dinner - in a similar way, taking a day off from tech makes it easier to resist the next day. And the more you do it, the more weeks you persist with taking a day off, the easier it gets and the looser the grip of addiction grows on both you and your family.

What about coffee and tea? Could you give up caffeine for a few hours? Of course you could - most of us realise that taking a hit of caffeine before bed is a poor idea - many of my friends don't drink caffeinated beverages after lunchtime.

Mind you, I'm of an age where I've moved from alcohol before bed, to coffee, to ginger tea, and I'm soon expecting cocoa or malt & milk drinks to come knocking at the door.

The problem with caffeine is that withdrawal comes with the physical discomfort of a headache, together with the personal discomfort of decaf not tasting as good. Caroline and I gave up caffeine when she was pregnant, and I can absolutely tell you that you will feel calmer without it if you give it a go. I cannot say that it's a habit that's persisted with us, but we go through cycles when we pull ourselves off it just to see if we can.

Do not try and take a day off without a plan. We did. I talked about it briefly in an earlier chapter, and now you need to think about what you can and cannot do.

The day before is just as important as the day itself. You may not realise it but there are certain things that are going to cause more temptation than others. We have three major pitfalls that we still occasionally forget:

Internet shopping for physical things. By this I mean act of purchasing something you 'need' - I'm thinking particularly of school supplies and food deliveries. Our family are great at the last minute stuff simply because we've become used to the next day delivery services and the abundance of choice. It is really easy to convince yourself that the food shop needs doing so you can save money and time, but that's not good.

Back in the olden days, shops closed on a Sunday. In fact they closed half way through Saturday and for a half day every week. People still went to work, but they had to plan around the shop opening and closing time. Although we have become used to everything when we want it, with no thought for other peoples working hours or inconvenience, it is possible to both plan ahead, and also to do without for a day.

Worst case scenario is that you have to leave your house and go and interact with someone at the local supermarket - but it's easier to get your shopping done the day before. Oh - and stay away from the 'self service' checkout - that counts as technology and internet enabled too.

The other one is more for the children than it is for the adults - although there are exceptions here too. Homework is the elephant in the room, both in terms of an evening off, and the whole day.

The very first time we took our 'day', it was during a school holiday. Despite the cataclysm, this certainly helped. Looking back, had homework become an issue then I suspect we may have given up then and there.

The week after our first day off, Saturday became internet bingeing day. I wasn't too concerned to be honest, I saw it as a natural reaction to an upcoming denial of service! Foolishly I thought that the family would also become sick of it - but that wasn't to be the case. That evening as curfew came in as expected - I'd like to think I breathed a sigh of relief at the upcoming day and a half without tech.

But I didn't - my own addiction started to make me anxious too. I took one last look at the news and weather - then placed my phone onto my study desk, and we enjoyed dinner and a movie as a family before heading off to bed.

The next day as we sat around the breakfast table, Ben told me that he needed to do some homework, and therefore couldn't be without the internet. Gabriel and Jessica said the same.

"But why didn't you do this yesterday?", I asked.

"We forgot".

Hmmm - I'll give the benefit of the doubt in retrospect, but my own short temper did not make the exchange that followed as constructive as it could have been. Regardless - I did not want them to get into trouble for missing homework deadlines, but another rule went into place.

As hard is was going to be - if homework didn't get done (at least the sort that requires internet access) before Sunday, then they were going to have to get into trouble, and Caroline and I would have to deal with the consequences of detentions and parent meetings.

That sounds like a tough line to take, and it is. But consider that if we were going to devote a day to going out to a theme park, or heading to a museum in the city, then 'somehow' the homework would get done during the week, or on the Saturday.

We had several family discussions around this particular topic, and it took several months before the ideal solution presented itself - which was for Caroline and I to ask for help doing various household chores on Saturdays. Doing homework allows you to be left in peace - 'playing' on the internet is an open invitation to parents that you have free time.

So if the dishwasher needs emptying, the clothes folding, the lawn mowing, or even if I need someone just to hand tools to me when I'm fixing things - the children get yanked from their comfortable spaces to lend a hand.

It seems that even homework is preferable to standing outside on a cold day at the bottom of a ladder, or making the beds, or sorting the washing out and it was amazing how quickly Sunday's became a homework free day again. This time with the added bonus that there's been a little more work ethic embedded in their lives.

Full disclosure here though - we do allow Ben to work in whatever way he needs for his exams, and the same is now true of Gabriel during revision time. We trust them not to move out of 'homework' to distraction and games, and I will periodically check on them. The alternative approach - placing more controls on their computers was seemingly impractical - as study and homework research can take you in many directions, but it is no where near as tough to do as you think, just experiment with parental and internet controls to find the right balance.

Every so often we 'test' the water to see if the family can be trusted with lower restriction - in effect self-regulate their own behaviour. Sometimes the outcome is good, sometimes not so much.

On one Sunday, a year or so into doing this, Caroline and I left the house, having disabled a bunch of internet destinations using our providers internet controls. We always have porn, nudity, drugs, self-harm and violence filters on, but we decided to add media streaming, game, social media and distraction sites, after all they shouldn't be on the web for anything other than homework purposes

Ben and Gabriel both confessed to noticing that we'd blocked the additional destinations, and were concerned this would be something of a 'permanent' event. We had a very mature chat about 'trust' and moved on.

If you want to try some 'custom' filters yourself, feel free to check out some of the technical sections at the back of the book.

Ah parental controls. Another area for potential controversy.

If you have read this far, and you've looked at the chapter on pornography, and you still think parental controls are a bad idea, then I'm going to respectfully disagree with you. There are a number of 'levels' of control you can impose.

At the first level, and this is a complete no-brainer, is to change your internet provider settings at source. In the UK, all internet providers provide this service. You can easily do this by logging into your provider account and setting it up.

I realise that if you want to engage in looking at pornography yourself this is going to be a challenge - but would you leave a pornographic magazine or a DVD out on display in your house for children to find? If the answer is 'no' and you don't have parental controls then ask yourself what the difference is between doing that, and leaving an unrestricted tablet around.

Entertainingly for us, British Telecom used to group the Windsor & Eton Brewery in the same threat category as PornHub - so when I wanted to order some beer, or look at a pub review I had to enter my password to provide a temporary exception.

(It should go without saying, but only a buffoon gives children their administrator passwords).

Parental controls will prevent the flow of most unsavoury content crossing the threshold. You may never stop it all - but you can eliminate most of it, and make it much, much harder to gain access to.

Realistically, you need to step this up by adding either vendor (Microsoft or Apple) parental controls to devices, setting safe search on web-browsers and investing in one of the many excellent solutions for managing it.

The counter argument to parental controls imposition is that you should be having conversations with your children to educate them, and while I agree with this I suspect that the eight year old in the earlier story who stumbled across necrophilia would not have heard about it from his parents.

I find it increasingly bizarre when people I speak with object to the idea of parental controls, they'll typically talk about trust, and civil liberty and any number of things - but I think it's far more to do with the fact that they feel technically under equipped to do so.

Yes - of course no child wants parental controls on their phone, their laptop, their tablet or their TV streaming - but I think Noah (my eight year old) would cheerfully get behind the wheel of a car and drive it, and we don't allow that either. The web IS a dangerous place - for so many reasons, and while education plays a major part in safety, there is still the need for adult supervision.

Oh, and yes - they can still use other peoples computers to see it - but porn surfing is not one of the most popular group activities among teenagers. Limitation and education are the best way forward.

Regardless of this - we're not talking exclusively about porn, we're talking about distraction, gaming and social media. It is possible to fine tune these on a case by case basis, but we found doing that was too time consuming and counter-productive.

And so we return to the day off and making that plan to reduce the stress (and the chances of success) - this is when the diet (and the associated hunger pains) start to kick in.

The easiest thing to do is to go out, leave the house and do your best to take yourself somewhere that you wouldn't normally make use of your tech. From experience, these are the places and activities that work best for us:

Best

Cinema

Swimming

Cycling

Church

The Pub

Gardening

Second best

Museums

Walking

Visiting parks

Visiting friends/grandparents

You'll probably have some additions - I have friends who regularly visit an artificial ski slope, which also strikes me as a rather challenging environment to use your smartphone in.

This isn't something to do every diet day, but for the first four weeks we'd strongly advise it as a method of relieving anxiety, simply due to the distraction effect and distancing from the temptation.

Also come to an agreement on what's going to happen to each device on the day. We found that (at least during the first few weeks) it was much easier to switch everything off - literally power down as much as we could - and that included all but one of the phones.

This works on a number of levels - firstly you make a mental commitment with the action of switching them off - not a big one, but it's far more effective than simply placing phones into airline mode and computers and consoles into standby or unplugging a network cable. You also avoid the need for any technical expertise at all.

This forces extra steps to succumb to temptation - flicking airline mode off doesn't really qualify as an inconvenience, but the few seconds it takes to reboot give everyone time to reflect on the fact that they are failing to give up for even a single day, and that can be all it takes to avoid the temptation.

The biggest inconvenience comes when we decide to sit down and watch a movie together - the router needs to go back on, sometimes the media server, and we have to wait literally minutes before the film is ready to go..........the agony of such a long wait!

In our house, we sometimes put the portable devices in a box - out of sight is out of mind, but we no longer switch them off, it's just a visible physical commitment that we're going 'dark' for a day.

Aside from getting out of the house, there are number of other things you can work on. Your brain is likely to be geared up to fill in spare time with technical activities, so 'free time' can be tough - but you need to accept that there is likely to be tension and fractious behaviour (remember our earlier chapter on withdrawal).

Board games can work - but it feels a little '1950's' to us, although we've come to enjoy them more recently as we sometimes have friends over to join in.

Pick a game that's going to work for you though - high conflict and long games didn't work for us at all, in fact it just made things worse. We'd advise avoiding Risk and Monopoly (at least for the first few weeks) - irritable and anxious people competing with each other is not good for harmony.

You'll also notice that your day seems longer, without the instant gratification and distraction, your mind is forced to find other things to do - in the case of our children, during the first few weeks it was 'argue as much as possible'.

No matter what happens on the first day, you will get a 'result' of some sort - if nothing changes, and nobody misses their gadgets at all then that is truly amazing. Please take the time to let me hear about it, because we've yet to see it in any of our friends.

It may sound obvious, but creating some kind of reward at the end of the day is going to help with adopting this as a habit. That can start on week one, but you're better waiting until the following week - no matter what you do on the first day, the reaction to withdrawal is likely to be different than in following weeks.

What do I mean by a 'reward'?   A trip out the cinema, the purchase of a new film, a slap up lunch at the burger chain of your choice - you know your own family. We found that a new movie to watch on the TV every week was one of the best things we could do - but we buy a physical copy earlier in the week so we have an 'artefact' around the house to look at.

Of course, we had none of these guidelines so our day was far, far different.....and one I never wish to repeat.

I don't want to pretend for a moment that we have this down to a fine art - after three years of practice, there are still slips. A few weeks ago my Wife had stepped out for some reason - and came back to find Gabriel had been unable to resist looking for a Spiderman t-shirt on Amazon, and Jessica had sent a few text messages to one of her friends. We talked it through, and for last few weeks we've gone back to 'router off, phones in a box'.

Digital Snooping

This brings us to another 'difficult' area for parents in particular - snooping on the behaviour of their children. This may be where our 7.6 strictness rating comes from but there are some basic rules of the internet that we have in place, which we like to call 'common sense'. These are:

No social media unless one or both parents are following you. This goes all the way up to 18 years of age - and hopefully will extend beyond.

No deleting browsing history. If you look at the browsing history on one of your families computers or phones, and there are 'holes' or 'nothing' then something is being hidden. Messing with browsing history is an instant seven day confiscation.

Password sharing for all devices (key codes, computers etc.) We make no secret of the fact that we check their computers and phones - it becomes a rarer occurrence as they get older, but the knowledge that we can plays an important part.

How can we enforce this? We pay the phone bills and provide the computers (not to mention food, lodging and heat).

You may think that this is an imposition on civil liberties, but let me give you a very graphic example of why this is not the case, using Jessica as an example.

A short time ago, her boyfriend posted a picture to Instagram of Jessica in a dress, it was a lovely picture and he put "Appreciation post for my girl" as the caption (don't judge the spelling, focus on the sentiment). Both of them have their accounts locked to ensure that only their friends can follow them, and both are aware that I expect to be able to see their activity. Again - they are 13 (Jessica was 12 at the time), and his parents do exactly the same.

As you can see from the screen capture below, the responses were mostly nice and funny - except for one. I'll draw your attention again to the fact that these are 12 and 13 year old children. The boy in question was entirely unknown to me, a friend of Jessica's beau - and he removed the post three minutes after I made mine.

Let's just leave aside the fact that many people saw the comment - and that Jessica clearly had heard such things before - and focus on the exact words used. Creepy in every way.

B.F. called Jessica to apologise on behalf of the offending individual, and blocked him.

Talking to her boyfriends parents a couple of days later, although they had missed this particular post, they did know the child who had made the comment - and in turn, had a conversation with his parents about it. The old saying "it takes a village to raise a child" seems just as applicable in the digital age.

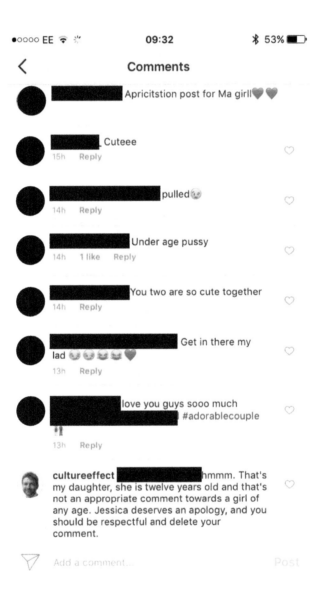

It would be naive to expect that we see everything our children see online, but a little parental supervision gives a measure of protection that is usually appreciated.

You have to decide where you draw that line - we have friends who allow no form of social media access at all - we also have friends that never check.

Onward - Weeks 2-4

It may be that after you've got through one full day of this, you decide not to do it any more. This diet may not be for you - but beware of what the trap of addiction and associated withdrawal symptoms pose to your decision making.

It's important to think hard about what you learned - if you couldn't make it through a day without hitting the tech, then regardless of the excuse you're now giving yourself you DO have a problem. You can decide to live with the problem, or not - that's up to you. Diets fail.

If, like us you decided that the pain and suffering caused by taking a day off was a very, very bad thing - then I'd advise you to press on. But be warned that at first it gets harder, not easier - because the temptation to cheat and conceal becomes very high.

Not just with the children either.

We're very lucky, Caroline could do without the internet and her phone. She doesn't particularly like using hers and if it wasn't for text messages to friends and emails for work could live without it easily. She is our failsafe and oversight in one lovely package - in the early months of our experiment she was the one who posed the toughest questions, and together we came up with the exceptions list you saw earlier.

Because I'm the biggest addict, I'm capable of spotting the violations earlier (because I'm tempted myself).

We found weeks 2-4 were the hardest, just as with every withdrawal process. There is no rocket science here though - it's a case of toughing it out and sticking to the rules. You'll know when the addiction is broken simply because everyone's mood will improve and the fighting against taking a day will stop.

A Week Off - The Detox

We went on a camping trip a few years ago as a family. Among all the camping gear, everyone brought phones and we also collected a few old Nintendo DS consoles and a tablet (for movies if the weather was bad).

As we were in the middle of our 'tech free day' experiment, we also decided to limit the consumption of our technology by refraining from bringing external power sources. The only way to charge anything was using the power socket in the car if we went out for the day. The only way to reach the internet was through the phone data plans, or ask to tether to the 'unlimited' plan on my phone.

But a strange and unexpected thing happened - after the second evening, nobody bothered with their technology. There were some early arguments and teenage tantrums during the first couple of days, but acceptance soon set in, and alternatives were found.

On the few rainy days we had, we found other stuff to do - heading to the cinema, spending more time in a cafe, or reading our books. We did find that our little battery powered radio became our most important contact point - providing news, weather and music throughout the holiday.

When we got home, there was no instant reflex to revert back to old habits, but the familiar environment, friends, work and expectations all conspired to return us to our old ways within a few weeks - but the memory of that lives on, and there are often times when we all think - "We could give this up completely". That's a nice feeling.

As with substance addiction, it seems that technological and internet addiction follow the same pattern. It's all very easy (if a little twitchy) at first, but within half a day the anxiety is boosted. The next few days are spent trying to find alternatives and other distractions, before the <u>need</u> starts to subside. After a week it's easy, but symptoms can persist for years. This is known as 'post-acute withdrawal syndrome'

Heroin Withdrawal Timeline

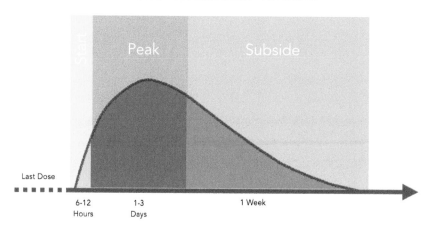

However, just like performing a food detox both the memory and the benefits live on.

In particular the knowledge that you <u>can</u> spend a week away can give you increased willpower to stop using short-term, and the mental benefits will allow you to think more clearly and socialise better.

Jessica went to a birthday party recently and got annoyed that many of her friends spent the evening 'looking down' at their phones, locked away in a world of their own. When the time came for her sleepover a few weeks later she removed the phones from her friends at the door, and announced to them that they were being locked away for the next 24 hours.

To my surprise, most of them didn't put up a fight - although one of the boys was hoisted into the air with a girl on each limb and his phone extracted forcibly.

The positive peer pressure throughout the evening kept them away from the internet, and only two exceptions occurred. One of the girls found a movie they were watching too scary, and the others allowed her the phone for an hour to distract her - after which it was returned to the lock box.

But another girl could not manage without it.

The first thing she asked for in the morning was her phone, and after 40 minutes of persistence the others agreed to let her have it. Despite all the peer pressure to stay away, she kept it stuck to her hand until she was collected. At one point she was tapping away at the breakfast table, and when asked by the others what she was doing said "homework", then promptly tucked it away under her leg - before taking it back out two minutes later.

Several of the parents have since told us that their children are asking for a weekly day off now.......

More Complex Temptations

Pokemon Go

In 2016 the game 'Pokemon Go' hit was earning more than $10m per day, and had 100m downloads in it's first month of release - it made a serious impact both on the gaming market and on our technical temptations.

As a family we all became slightly besotted with it for different reasons, although Caroline's phone was hijacked by Noah in order for him to join in with the fun.

This was a game that you couldn't sit inside and play - and although there had been others, this one caught the imagination of a broad swathe of players who had grown used to a series of Pokemon trading cards, cartoons and games over two decades.

In the Pokemon Go world, your smart phone acted as a window to unseen creatures - with a tracking radar - taking to the streets and fields with phone in hand gave you a chance to catch all manner of weird and wonderful beasts, and then evolve them, fight with and collect them. The more you walked, the more rewards and creatures you received.

For us, this gave a great level of entertainment - with five phones and a relatively active lifestyle we found ourselves dashing about catching the things on most days - the children got home from school and scampered outside to see what they could find, and on some weekends got together with friends at local towns to play as a group.

In the village where I live, it became 'normal' to see new groups of people hanging about together. Socially, it certainly changed things - when the servers crashed on the game, all over the world people were still congregating in public areas as they had grown used to talking, and had made new friends.

As the months went by, more and more studies showed that there were health benefits too - despite the occasional accident as somebody chased a creature into the sea, it transpired that more and more steps were being recorded, and the health benefits that came with increased exercise seemed to follow.

A Stanford University/Microsoft study in October 2016 looked at 31,793 Microsoft band users, and identified 1,420 who were Pokemon Go players. Looking at the "before and after" data, analysis showed that on average the players increased their daily step count by more than 25% - the authors estimate that during the 30 days of the study, over 144 billion steps were added to the US population by Pokemon Go players. A pattern mirrored by my own Fitbit.

Not only was this free to download game promoting some social interaction, it was also improving fitness levels, health and life expectancy - and engaging previously inactive gamers in exercise.

Gamification of exercise is an ongoing trend, apparently I've walked the length of India and climbed well over the height of clouds in the last year. I love this stuff, and competing with my friends on weekly challenges does increase my activity for sure (although I never check on a Sunday).

But his did cause a challenge for us - especially once our children returned to school. During the summer vacation, it was easy. They could play all day run around and go crazy - after 7pm and on Sundays, the rules applied - and although there were some complaints about missing out - we dealt with it.

However school time doesn't give a lot of opportunity, and we found that there was much more chance of the children happily joining us on a long walk on Sunday if they could 'walk their eggs' (more walking means creatures hatch from eggs - and catch monsters.

Truthfully - I enjoyed playing the game too, and it became a family event to walk the dog and play Pokemon. For the <u>most</u> part we were successful at avoiding the alerts and mundane temptations as we'd become used to temporary abstinence. As ever though, it was Caroline who spotted the problem - as we wandered around with our heads down, we'd started to immerse ourselves in the virtual world and withdraw from the real one.

For sure, we were all having fun at the start, chatting and running and catching - but after a while it became 'habit' - the conversation died, the phone was stuck in hand, and we became the tech zombies that were trying not to emulate. Of course, anxiety levels rose with the technology and the 'barely open door' to the rest of the internet world. Why not check the weather? It's just a click away - oh look at that text message, I should respond to that email……..

So the phones went away once again.

Television

What defines TV? Different age groups, different eras, different ideas. Friends and family research would lead me to believe that 70+ generally accept that TV comes through an aerial (or a cable) and can be found on a small number of channels, and although the video cassette recorder has joined the dinosaurs, the new box will allow hundreds of hours of recording. Most of which will never be watched.

40+ generally accept that there are hundreds of channels and make use of them, but still record what's missed in an effort to stock up a local film library and some additional TV for when boredom strikes.

30+ make good solid use of TV online services, catch up through the websites of their favourite channels, record some stuff and stream more.

Under 30? TV is a joke. There is no such thing - a 'TV' is a screen for showing what you want, when you want it. Sometimes this may be with other people, sometimes on your own. Sometimes on your computer, laptop, tablet or phone. It's just as likely to find online streaming being watched (I mean YouTube or similar), or Netflix series than actually broadcast through the 'regular' TV network.

In the UK, children's TV was moved from BBC1 and 2 to

Cbeebies and CBBC in 2007. The reason? Research showed that children wanted more focused TV, and adults didn't want nothing to watch at 4pm in the afternoon on the main channels. They also found much of the content consumed by under 11's was online through their existing BBC sites - and so the old fashioned habit of settling down on the sofa to watch kids television with parent or siblings was lost and divided - older kids to one room for CBBC, younger to another of CBeebies, adults to another for BBC1.

And we lost something of our family social interaction at that point. And it gets to be a greater challenge with the 'on demand' entertainment world that we now find ourselves part of. Because now you can watch what you like, when you like, wherever you like.

I love a good binge watch as much as anyone. Sitting through hours of the most popular TV is great fun - 'Stranger Things' on Netflix particularly captured our hearts recently - but there are two things that I really, really miss and I mourn it's loss for the children too.

How about anticipation? Waiting a week before the next episode of these things is great - and provides a few additional benefits too - discussing it with friends who also watched it the night before (Lost, Game of Thrones, 24). The absolute finality of knowing there is no more and going to bed, rather than staying up until 2am to watch the next four episodes. With a streaming series, there is no 'cliffhanger' that cannot be overcome, and that's sad.

Something that also gets missed is 'accidental' learning. Watching things you know you like leads to consumption of the same entertainment - we occasionally experiment with only watching one 'regular' TV channel during our curfews, and it works really, really well.

Everyone in our household loves a nature documentary - especially if Sir David Attenborough is involved. Blue Planet, Planet Earth etc. will enrapture us all, youngest to oldest - and yet we found ourselves recording it, planning to watch it later, and never watching it.

This is because it's easier to get into the habit of grabbing something for a short term, familiar hit online than it is to 'just watch what's on' - especially when the children complain that they "don't want to watch it because they've never seen it before."

We've come across all kinds of fantastic new things this way - and we've learned a lot too.

Friends Houses

How does this work when we go to friends houses, either as a family or individuals? At the start of our journey we noticed a slight increase in time spent around at friends, but nothing significant - and this has settled back into a more regular pattern.

Just as in all things, we cannot impose rules and regulations on the children when they are in someone else's care. What we can do is explain to them why we do spend time away from the tech, and hope that some of that sticks.

If they spend days away, then they will use the internet at their friends houses - but in a more sociable, group environment. There is a difference between sitting alone in your room on the web, and gaming with three friends - it's not perfect, but it is reality.

We were at a gathering recently, both Jessica and Gabriel were there too, and it amused all the parents to see Jessica appear in the living room at around 8pm with a handful of phones she had collected. She'd become fed up with sitting in a room with everyone 'face down' at their phones, and decided that she would collect them up and move them out of sight (along with her own phone). It didn't take long before worried young teenagers started drifting around looking for them - a kind of 'addicts' hide and seek.

The reverse is also true, when friends come over they find that there's no ability to jump online - but it's rarely a problem as we're all doing other things. There are definitely some confused looks at first, and ours can feel a little left out when their friends disappear into a quiet corner with their phone in hand, but it tends to take care of itself, and serves as a useful reminder of just how addicted it's possible to be. We find it amusing to move others phones around within the room, and watch the look of panic appear and the rapid head movements as they try to locate it.

Technical Stuff

This final section is for the technophobes, or those that want to know just a little bit more about some of the simple stuff you can do that you may think is complex. It's a short guide to some of the technical skills you really should have in todays world - think of it as the electronic equivalent of learning to drive a car.

Router

This little box sits near the phone line in your house. It takes the signal in from the outside world (usually through a wire) and then beams it around your home in the form of wi-fi. In some homes, the router is joined by a cable to another router (something like an Apple Airport extreme).

To sever the internet in your house, all you have to do is switch off the router - it may have an on/off switch on it, or you can simply unplug it from the wall.

Do not worry about doing this. When you turn it on again, it may take a couple of minutes to get everything sorted, but it will come back.

Some routers allow you to set time limits on them. To do this you'll need to connect using an IP address. You can probably find this info in a user guide, but it's likely to look something like this -

192.168.1.254. The last number changes a bit.

If you type these numbers into your web browser, you'll get access to all kinds of fun stuff such as automatically switching off access at certain times, and blocking other computers from accessing the internet. This is a lot of fun, but you need to be a little patient and a little careful - different access limits can be set for every different device in the house. You will also need to reset the administrator password so your children/friends/parents don't go and change things without you knowing.

Content Filtering

Most internet providers allow the option of blocking 'bad stuff' at source. Experience dictates that this could be easier to find, as it is in the best interest of your provider to allow access to all content for various reasons including advertising revenue and revenue from usage.

Blocking stuff at source does mean that you also will not be allowed to see 'bad stuff' - although you can use you administrator password to lift restrictions temporarily. This is not something I would advise doing (did you read the section on porn?) - but our internet provider amusingly considers sites containing information on alcohol at the same level of risk as sites containing naked people.

You can also usually add things to 'exceptions' to allow or deny specific sites. If you simply cannot bring yourself to leave any particular website alone, you may choose to enter the details here.

Frankly, if you have children in the house, then you should be doing this. It's simple, straightforward and will provide a barrier which should deter most from seeing the worst parts of the web.

Parental Controls

Oh no, I couldn't possibly do that!

Yes you can, and you should. You may find that some parental controls are also available through your mobile provider (see content filtering above) - but you also have a lot of other options depending on the technology you use.

Both PC's and Mac's carry a pretty comprehensive and easy to use parental control system that will let you block content, approve applications before they are downloaded, and generally lock down devices and internet to a safe level. Microsoft currently call that "Family Security", Apple go with "Parental Controls".

These tools can be used not only to limit content, but also to limit screen time - which is a really effective way of introducing tech curfews that go beyond the internet. Yes, we've used these too - it works, although they are not popular. Do we still use them? Not as much - but we're accustomed to the diet, and trust now plays a part.

It's NOT hard to set these things up - if you can use the satnav in your car, and the TV in your living room you can probably work it out. Step up, and get it done. Just don't ask the children for help!

You can also use other software if you have a varied tech stack - if you're using some PC's, Android phones, Mac's and iPhones then you'll have your work cut out doing stuff to all of them. I cannot recommend any in particular, but there are a number of good options which a search for "Family internet safety software" will show you.

Social Media

Basic common sense here. If you are going to let your children out into the social media world, then you need to do two things.

You need to "follow" them, and they need to make sure their account is private. This means that the entire world cannot see what they are posting without asking for permission to see it first. Have a really good talk with them about how having less 'friends' is a good idea - if your child has 1000 followers on Facebook, you have a problem.

Of course they can get clever and set up two profiles in the hope that you won't find the other one - but you should be able to spot this. If the profile you're connected to has little activity then they are probably away doing other things using an account you don't know about.

The second thing to do, which may seem a little more awkward (but shouldn't be), is to regularly sit with them and go through their phone and computer. Looking at their social media activity and talking through when you think they are getting it wrong.

Don't be fooled by the 'digital natives' mantra - you wouldn't drop your kids in the jungle and hope they will survive - you need to be active in helping them.

There are plenty of social media trends on the go at any one time - right now

Facebook (pictures and conversations),

Twitter (short conversations and pictures),

YouTube (videos and comments),

Instagram (pictures and some conversations),

LinkedIn (grown ups and jobs)

Snapchat (enhanced texting with fun stuff)

are the ones you've probably heard of, but there are many others including Pinterest, Tumblr, Reddit, Flickr, VK and Vine.

What you may not realise is that Facebook is relatively 'clean' - they are quick to remove naked people and most other offensive content. Instagram falls into the same category. Twitter is NOT clean - search for anything and you will find it. Amusingly, the best way to find pornography in Instagram is to use emoji's. The world has gone mad.

Of course, the predominant social media platform for anyone is the one that their friends are using - in the early days of Snapchat, the application was abused and allowed for easy online bullying by groups. As messages disappear after a short period of time, it allowed for images and text to be sent without fear of further sharing or recording. Sadly, many children (and adults) overlooked the ability of most devices to screenshot, which led to inappropriate and private images being used for blackmail purposes. Snapchat have taken measures to address this, and now users get a message if somebody uses the device to screenshot - but of course anyone can take a photograph of a screen with another device.

So it was with some trepidation that I approved Jessica and Gabriel to use Snapchat, and I ask to see the conversations on a regular basis. We speak at length on the dangers of sharing information and images online, and I would hope that they will not be foolish enough to post anything that they would not be happy with me, their mother or their grandparents seeing.

Cyber Bullying

My last word is reserved for the very serious subject of cyber-bullying. An ugly truth of the modern world is that bullying can now be inflicted from afar, by many. When it happens to adults, it tends to be called 'trolling' - but that's simply concealing reality. Adults can be bullied too.

There could be a whole book on this one subject in particular - but having dealt with this for several adult friends, and several children too here is some direct advice.

1   Being picked on is bad. It hurts. But it's not worth harming yourself. There are far too many examples of people being driven to suicide by emotional, physical or financial blackmail. For example, somebody may have a picture or video of you with no clothes on. Yes it's really embarrassing - but it will pass. Be careful with what you post and share, and you can minimise the risk.

2   The social media providers are good at dealing with this kind of thing. Notifying the good people at Facebook that there is a post which contains nudity, bullying etc. will have that person's content removed. Yes - they may still put it up somewhere else under a different profile, but eventually they will give up.

3 Report it to the police. There may not be much that they can do, but in many cases a visit from a man with a scary uniform is all it takes to shut down the behaviour. And let the right people know at school (if it's your child).

4 Remember that even if you made a mistake, nobody deserves to be bullied, victimised or otherwise 'trolled' by anybody else. You can relieve the pressure on yourself by telling those around you what is going on - in the Ashley Madison example the best advice was to tell your partner immediately. Confess, beg forgiveness, and prevent the risk of blackmail.

And Finally

I hope that this book has inspired you to reduce your internet consumption - or at the very least see how it feels to break the addiction chains (even if only for a short time), then take a step back and gain a slightly different perspective on your behaviour and that of your family.

'They' say that every journey begins with a single step - the first of these is to ignore all your own arguments for not taking a break and just do it.

If you can persuade everyone in your family to read this book, then you'll have an easier time bringing everyone else with you on the journey - if not, then you'll need to be an evangelist, diplomat, dictator, persuader and educator (which is pretty much the definition of a parent I think).

Hopefully you have enjoyed reading 'Digitox', and picked up some interesting facts to share across the dinner table with family and friends - but I have greater hope that you'll take what you've learned here, change your life for the better and pass on the habit to those around you.

Let me know how you get on.

About The Author

Mark was given his first computer (a BBC Micro) aged 10, played a few basic games, and started programming it shortly afterwards in an attempt to create better ones. After graduating with a first class honours degree in Business Studies & Technology he joined Dun & Bradstreet and has spent over two decades in the IT software industry, working all over the world and accumulating nearly two million air miles.

He now spends time helping large innovative corporations get the best from their people as a leadership & culture consultant, and shares his experiences at Oxford Brookes University as an associate lecturer.

He has been married to his beautiful Wife Caroline for twenty years, and together they have four children and a dog called Shelby. Everyone in the family (including the dog) is blond except him, which is slightly confusing and also quite sad, as he ruins the aesthetic of every group photograph.

His best friend is a sarcastic Welshman whose proudest achievement is the creation of a gourmet recipe for 'cheese on plate'. Don't ask. Just don't.

Acknowledgements

This book would not have been possible without the support of so many people. I'm sure to miss a few, and for that I sincerely apologise.

First and foremost the biggest thank you goes (of course) to my family. Despite their sometimes unwilling participation in restrictions, experiments and discussions this would never have been possible without their support, patience and feedback. Not to mention having to suffer through my many grumpy writers block moments, and my own withdrawal challenges.

The first person to suggest writing a book about our experiences was Liggy Webb, not only an outstanding author, but one of the loveliest and most generous people I know. For suggestions, edits, feedback and friendship I cannot thank her enough.

For the final push, when I had all but given up, I have to thank the person that pestered and nagged me the most, Emma Taylor from the Leadership Whisperers (yes that pun is intentional - they work with horses), and her business partner and author Jude Jennison.

Ian Sutherland, an IT industry guru and best selling crime thriller writer stepped in with lots of free advice on the mechanics of the book industry, following an introduction from my good friend and mentor Chris Miller. Without the two of them, this manuscript would still be sitting on my desk.

To Ben Cameron and the brilliant team at Cameron Publicity & Marketing I owe a huge debt of thanks for not only helping get the word out, but for also experimenting on their own families to see what would happen.

Welsh John and Texan John have supported me in so many ways it's hard to list. Thanks in particular to the Welshman for his obsessive word checking and edits, and the Texan for care packages from across the Atlantic and helping me tweak the copy for US readers.

My other proof readers acted as an impromptu editing team, going above and beyond what was asked - so to my parents, to Erika Biscoe and to Kay Bishop, all of whom suffered with early versions, thank you for your patience.

The amazing Cassie Peterson provided the musical backdrop to my writing. Charming, calming, soothing and inspiring in equal measure, her talent is boundless.

Last, and by no means least I would like to end this book the way it began. With thanks to you, the reader - who bravely picked up (or downloaded) a book that offered the promise of changing things for the better.